TAROT

TAROT

Naomi Ozaniec

TEACH YOURSELF BOOKS

Acknowledgements
Illustrations from Zolar Astrological Fortune Telling cards reproduced by permission of
U.S. Games Systems, Inc., Stamford, CT 06902 USA.
Copyright © 1983 by U.S. Games Systems, Inc. Further reproduction prohibited.

Cover photo reproduced with permission of Accademia Carrara di Belle Arti Bergamo.

For UK order queries: please contact Bookpoint Ltd, 39 Milton Park, Abingdon, Oxon
OX14 4TD. Telephone: (44) 01235 400414, Fax: (44) 01235 400454. Lines are open from
9.00 to 6.00, Monday to Saturday, with a 24 hour message answering service.
Email address: orders@bookpoint.co.uk

For USA & Canada order queries: please contact NTC/Contemporary Publishing, 4255
West Touhy Avenue, Lincolnwood, Illinois 60646–1975, USA. Telephone: (847) 679 5500,
Fax: (847) 679 2494.

Long renowned as the authoritative source for self-guided learning – with more than 30
million copies sold worldwide – the *Teach Yourself* series includes over 200 titles in the
fields of languages, crafts, hobbies, sports, and other leisure activities.

A catalogue record for this title is available from The British Library.

Library of Congress Catalog Card Number: 98-65903

First published in UK 1998 by Hodder Headline Plc, 338 Euston Road, London NW1 3BH.

First published in US 1998 by NTC/Contemporary Publishing, 4255 West Touhy Avenue,
Lincolnwood (Chicago), Illinois 60646–1975 USA.

The 'Teach Yourself' name and logo are registered trade marks of Hodder & Stoughton Ltd.

Typeset by Transet Limited, Coventry, England.
Printed in Great Britain for Hodder & Stoughton Educational, a division of Hodder
Headline Plc, 338 Euston Road, London NW1 3BH by Cox & Wyman Ltd, Reading,
Berkshire.

Impression number   10 9 8 7 6 5 4 3 2 1
Year   2003 2002 2001 2000 1999 1998

CONTENTS

INTRODUCTION

Tarot continues to grow in popularity. New packs continue to emerge. The fascination with Tarot seems inexhaustible. In an age of images and moving pictures, our need to find meaningful images is as real as ever. The fleeting image and the contrived icon do not satisfy the soul but merely appeal to the senses in a brief encounter. The images of the Tarot hold our interest, feed the mind and nourish the soul. The Tarot shows us images that sustain.

The Tarot gives us far more than is commonly supposed. So often the Tarot is associated only with prediction. A dubious reputation has grown from tales of its unnerving accuracy. In truth such accuracy is only a reflection of the reader. There is no doubt that Tarot lures with its predictive possibilities. If you are content with such a catch, you will find what you seek. But if your mind is curious, you will find a longer and more meaningful journey in the images of life.

Tarot can take you on a personal journey of exploration. You will find psychology, psychotherapy, mythology, meditation, spiritual philosophy, numerology, astrology and symbology. You will find the archetypes of the ages. You will find profound ideas expressed silently, not in words but in pictures. Entering this greater realm of Tarot requires interaction. The subtle alchemy of personal interaction will bring you closer to yourself. Here is the real treasure which is Tarot. Discover it for yourself if you wish. The invitation stands ever open. You alone will decide how far to journey in the company of the Tarot. It might prove to be an interesting and stimulating companion, a wise guide and even a lifelong friend.

How to use this book

This book is about the Tarot but at its heart it is about you. The book does not provide long lists of meanings in the hope that you will remember them. Teaching yourself Tarot is a more subtle and deeper process of assimilation than mere memory. The images and symbols that you see in front of you as Tarot cards need to be planted and internalised in your consciousness. The book offers a number of meditative experiences which together construct an inner vocabulary. If you are to teach yourself, you need to establish an organic and committed relationship with the Tarot. You will become engaged in the process of your own change. The symbols of the Tarot are deeply transformative; teaching yourself Tarot will undoubtedly bring about change. You will undergo transformation as you internalise the images of Tarot.

The book presents you with principles which you can apply and elaborate for yourself. Although people most often come to Tarot with expectations of 'reading the tarot', it has to be said that a much deeper and more sustaining current runs underneath the surface. The book presents many opportunities to enter into the inner philosophy of the Tarot. Use them as you wish, after all you are ultimately your own teacher. The book sets out to empower you as the active and involved reader. You can truly teach yourself Tarot.

1 | THE ROOTS OF TAROT

In the beginning was the symbol.
Dori Gombold, *The Psychodynamic Effects of Tarot Symbolism*

The human mind rejoices in symbolic forms, it has always done so. From the earliest beginnings to the latest explorations into space, the symbolic has served to express what we feel about ourselves. The message carried by SETI into the far reaches of space is a deliberate and specific statement of human existence. Perhaps it will be found and decoded as we too have found and decoded the symbolic statements of peoples and civilisations who dwelt on the earth before us. Marks, notches, paintings, representations, artefacts, images, icons and structures are the symbolic expressions of human experience. The Tarot is a symbol system too. The symbol provides an expansive metaphor, it captures a universal truth in a non-verbal form. The importance given to deductive reasoning has deadened our symbolic awareness. Our collective forgetting makes a personal rediscovery all the more delightful and exciting.

The attempt to validate the significance of Tarot by seeking its roots in the dim mists of time is quite unnecessary. We do not need to search for imagery in ancient temples in order to believe in Tarot. We do not need to hunt for glyphs in ancient caves in order to validate Tarot. We do not need to ransack the past in order to assign meaning to Tarot. Antiquity is no guarantee of anything other than age. The universal requires no validation – how could it? We do not need to prove the existence of the sky, the rising of the Sun, the falling of rain. These are universal truths which are apparent to all. A child's picture of the sky is but one representation of this truth which could also take numerous other forms. The truth is changeless, its expression is infinite. The Zen arts of calligraphy, flower arranging, swordsmanship and archery seem to have little in common. Yet each has been used as a path to enlightenment. Each has been used as a vehicle for awakening, the enlightenment experience itself. The Great Teaching fits numerous containers. The Tarot is a container, it is a vehicle for spiritual awakening. We can look at swordsmanship as a martial art. We can look at calligraphy as a writing art. We can look at flower arranging as a decorative art. We can look at archery as a competitive art. We can look at all of these as forms which carry the artless art, the art of waking. We can look at Tarot as a game. We can look at Tarot as a form which carries universal truth, the Ancient and Perennial Wisdom. We always see what we want to see, neither more nor less.

The exoteric history: the outer game

What else do they mean, The Magician and The Fool, other than they be swindler and the trickster? What other meaning have the Popess, The Chariot, The Traitor, The Wheel, The Hunchback, Strength, The Star, The Sun, The Moon and Hell and all the rest of the motley crew?

Flavio Alberti Lollio, *Invettiva contra Il Giuoco del Tarocco*

The familiar card pack of four suits appeared in Europe in about 1377. It is difficult to state conclusively whether this was an independent invention or a European development of an oriental pastime as gaming certainly existed at an early date in China. Some 60 years after the first European pack, a new set of cards emerged, cards with trumps, *carte da trionfi*. This contained a separate suit of Trumps, or Triumphs, and included an additional picture card in each of the four suits. Michael Dummet, author of *The Game of Tarot*, pays compliment to the originality of the new game: 'The invention of the Tarot pack was one of the great moments in the history of card play'.[1] It seems most likely that *carte da trionfi* originated in one of the Italian courts. Michael Dummet favours the d'Este court of Ferrara among the competing claims of Bologna and Milan. The playful, romantic, pleasure loving life at this court suggests the perfect ambience for the creation of a new game. Moreover, the earliest reference to these new cards appears in 1442 in the account books from Ferrara. The *Registro dei Mandati* mentions *pare uno de carte da trionfi*, a pack of cards with trumps. The *Registro di Guardaroba* includes a record of the purchase of *quattro paia di carticelle da trionfi*. Coincidentally another set of cards was also in evidence during this period. Often but misleadingly called the *Tarocchi of Mantegna* these cards have now been attributed to

Parrasio Michele of Ferrara. The set consisted of 50 cards in five classes of ten cards depicting The Conditions of Man, The Muses and Apollo, The Liberal Arts, Cosmic Principles and finally the Firmament of the Universe. From the outset these cards were most probably used to instruct in philosophical and moral principles. Some of the characters shown here were to reappear as the 22 Triumphs when game and philosophy blended seamlessly into one another. The actual term *tarocchi* as distinct from *carte da trionfi*, was recorded in one of the account books of Ferrara dating from 1516. The word *tarocchi* came into general use and supplanted the earlier and looser description.

We do not currently think of Tarot as a card game like whist or bridge but there is no doubt that precursors of the cards that we now know as Tarot enjoyed an earlier incarnation as a card game. It was described in 1659 in the French book of games, *La Maison Academique de Jeux*. The instructions and descriptions finally disappeared from the manual in 1718. We do not have any actual descriptions of Tarot as a game before the middle of the seventeenth century though it is possible to reconstruct the main features of the earlier game with a fair degree of certainty. As a game Tarot fits into the category of trick taking games like whist. In other words the highest ranking card wins the trick. It seems most likely that Tarocchi was a game for three persons and was played in a counter-clockwise direction. As with all trick taking games every player followed suit. The Trump cards were ranked in numerical order, Trump XXI commonly being the highest. To add to the excitement of the game, in the suits of Swords and Batons, the tens were the highest and the aces were the lowest but in the suits of Coins and Cups, the aces ranked high and tens ranked low. The court were cards ranked in the order we would expect, the king followed by the queen, the cavalier and then the jack (or maid). Additionally some cards carried points, usually Trumps I and XXI and the court cards. The Fool had a special significance. It released the player from having to follow suit. In the French game it was laid with the words 'the fool serves as excuse' or simply 'l'excuse'. Tarocchi was clearly a game demanding some concentration. If you can put all your contemporary esoteric conceptions to one side, you might like to try an evening of Tarocchi, the game.

The light within the court at Ferrara was not to last. The fun loving freedom was merely loaned along with fiefdom and in 1597 it was reclaimed by the papal realm. The playful court faded under its less than jovial new ownership. Until the demise of the Ferrara court, a spirit of friendly rivalry between Bologna, Ferrara, Florence and Milan prevailed. Each of the centres developed a slightly different version of the game. The Trumps were not originally numbered so there remained a great deal of scope for individual style and further invention. Each centre ranked the Trumps in their own way. In the Ferrarese style of play, Trump XXI, the World, was the highest Trump. In the Bolognese version Trump XX remained the highest. Ferrara was the first to introduce numbered Trumps in the late fifteenth century, but in the Bologna game no numbers were introduced until the second half of the eighteenth century. Local variations included different scoring systems. The Bolognese Tarocchi awarded points to Trump XX, the Angel (the contemporary 'Judgement'). There was not one game of Tarocchi but several, each evolving under its own impetus. Bologna in fact developed its own particular game known as *tarocchino*, a diminutive version of Tarocchi which used only 62 cards by omitting four numerals from each suit. By the end of the fifteenth century the Bolognan game spread to Florence. Here the game underwent a radical transformation and a new game emerged. The Florentines dropped the Papess, converted the Pope to another Emperor and increased the Trumps to 40 with the addition of the 12 signs of the zodiac, the four elements, and the Virtues, namely Charity, Faith, Prudence and Hope. This made a total of 97 cards. The new game was called *germanini* or later *minchiate*. The game spread throughout Tuscany, the papal states and Genoa but it never gained the popularity of Tarocchi, mainly due to the unwieldy number of cards in the pack. In 1752 under pressure from the papacy, the four cards, Pope, Papess, Emperor and Empress known collectively as *papi,* were replaced by four Moorish kings.

It was the Milanese game which spread into France and Switzerland as a result of French invasion and occupation of Milan. Cross-cultural fertilisation began to work and France made its own significant contribution to the development of Tarot. The *Tarot de Marseilles* included the names of the Trumps and court cards for the first time. Piedmontese cardmakers adapted the French form and gave it a distinctive character now known as *Tarocchi Piedmontese*. In about 1740 Bolognese cardmakers also adopted the French innovation and translated the French names back into Italian. In this to and fro across time and geographical borders, Tarocchi took on new clothes. In another cross-cultural interchange when the card making industry of Lombardy declined during the seventeenth century, cards were imported from France. By 1595 cards were being manufactured in Paris and by 1599 at Nancy. In 1603 the manufacturers of Lyons even tried to suppress the rising success of manufacture in the city of Marseilles. The attempt failed and in 1631 Marseilles received a royal edict for its activities. The Tarot was an expanding business. Rouen and Lyons became the export centres for England, Portugal, Spain, Flanders and Switzerland. The Tarot of Marseilles remained popular. Following the Second World War, the game was revived through the popular *Tarot de Marseilles*. The recorded history of Tarot provides a fascinating glimpse into people and places, trade and art, commerce and leisure, state and province.

Gaming has always enjoyed a dangerous reputation. The gaming table has been beloved of the reckless, the optimistic, the hopeful and the carefree while assuming monstrous guise for the puritanical and strait-laced. In 1550 Flavio Alberti Lollio published a general invective against gaming in general and Tarocchi in particular.

Evil game, perfidious and false, game that squanders your money, game that would impoverish Atlas and Midas, since it is the cousin of the Bassetta: And while man hopes to derive pleasure from it, it always keeps him in pain and fear. Now the cards are being dealt: the first hand appears good, so you accept the invitation and you play again: the ones that follow show a new face, but they no longer care about your affairs: and thus you are left rather suspended: the other player believing himself to be favoured by the cards will raise the stakes: then, pierced with shame, grief, envy and anger, you throw in your hand with lowered head come to naught.

Such a man does not feel any lesser sorrow than a captain, who believing he has won the battle, cries out Victory, Victory but sees by a counterattack that his men are defeated and dispersed.

Thereupon two new hands follow, now good, now poor and when you are waiting for the last one which might aid you, having already invited it, you see coming to you (alas, great pain) such raffish cards as may kill you, the complete opposite of your needs. So you are inflamed with pique, and while wrought with spite, you grudgingly pick up the remaining cards which are twenty. These fill your hands and for a long while they give you toil and trouble in arranging Money, Clubs, Cups and Swords and Triumphs. They must be put in order one by one, as a good shepherd who, having many sheep gathers them into separate flocks.

Lollio concluded his tirade with a heartfelt prayer.

Meanwhile I fondly pray, with offerings and vows to the gods in heaven, that they cause all ink to vanish at once: the yellow, the green, the white, the red and all the other colours by which Tarocco are made; that they make all paper go up in smoke and that no one ever be found who dares to carve designs in wood by which the cards are made; so that this art so damaging and evil shall be at once wiped from people's hearts and that posterity shall find no trace of it, and forever its memory will be obliterated.[2]

Poor Lollio would turn in his grave if he could see how his prayers for the obliteration of Tarot have been answered!

To understand the popularity of Tarot as a courtly game we need only recall the life of the times. The Triumphs merely mirrored the world at large. The Emperor was no distant imaginary figure but a world player of the time. The knights, kings, queens and pages were familiar characters from the backdrop of political intrigue which was ever present in royal circles. The court cards had a present meaning for those living the courtly life. Swords and staves, cups and gold coins were the stuff of ordinary life. The characters and content of Tarocchi were a familiar description of Renaissance life. As every age sees only its own reflection, so contemporary commentators saw the affairs of the times in the images of Tarocchi. Some saw the social fabric of the world in the four suits. The suits of swords represented the knights, nobility and aristocracy. Staves represented the peasantry. The suit of coins represented the commercial classes. Galcottus Martius writing between 1488 and 1490 referred to the four suits as spears, swords, cups and country loaves of bread. He related the suit of swords to the death of those who become mad over gaming. He saw staves or batons as instruments of punishment as they commonly were at that time. For Martius, the suit of cups represented the disputes of gamesters, while the suit of coins or bread represented sustenance through food and play. Covarrubias, writing in the early seventeenth century, suggested that the four suits represented the most hurtful and mortal dangers to mankind. The club represented the unsophisticated but effective weapon. The sword represented a more advanced weapon. The suits of coins and cups represented the causes of men's grievance, the drinking cup and the pouch of coins. Others saw the suits as emblems of the four virtues; Justice being the suit of swords, Fortitude the suit of clubs, Faith being the suit of cups and finally Charity being the suit of coins. Other commentators saw social forms in the courtly characters; the kings represented the power of the government, the queens represented religious belief, the knights represented history and the pages represented the arts and sciences. We currently see the four suits in terms of the Jungian functions of sensation, thinking, feeling and intuition. This is the mirror of the times in which we live.

The Visconti-Sforza families

The history of Tarot is also the history of particular individuals. The new game of Tarocchi came to serve a particular family tree. Now we glimpse a different courtly life through the Visconti and Sforza families. Our attention moves from the fun loving court of Ferrara to the dark intrigues at Milan. The name Sforza is itself a nickname meaning 'force', an epithet which sets the scene for us. The first duke of Milan was Bernabo Visconti. This Visconti was a ruthless tyrant who used every means at his disposal to secure his position of wealth, power and influence. He wedded his legitimate daughters to kings, dukes and counts. His less well placed illegitimate daughters were married to powerful soldiers of fortune, *condotierre* who waged war on their father-in-law's behalf in return. It is perhaps one of life's ironies that the name of Bernabo Visconti is remembered more in relation to the Tarot cards that bear his family name and less for his self-serving exploits. Like many tyrants before him Bernabo was deposed by an ambitious and even more despotic nephew. The nephew Giangaleazzo fathered two sons. The first of these, Giovanni Maria came to an untimely end when he was assassinated. The younger, Filippo also maintained the family style by marrying a woman twice his age in order to secure the loyalty of her dead husband's troops. Her usefulness outlived, she was beheaded in 1418 on trumped up charges of adultery. In 1423 his mistress produced a daughter who was named Bianca Maria Visconti. She was betrothed at the tender age of nine to Francesco Sforza, a *condottiere* some 22 years her senior. They were married in 1441 and – miracle of miracles – the marriage was long and happy. When

Filippo died without heir, the duchy was empty and waiting. The strong man Francesco claimed his father-in-law's title and secured it by force when he conquered Lombardy city by city. When Milan surrendered in 1450 he declared himself to be the fourth Duke of Milan. He had won by might, not by hereditary right. Having achieved his kingdom he ruled peacefully and efficiently for 16 years. He was succeeded firstly by his elder son, the cruel and dissolute Galeazzo who was assassinated and next by his grandson Giangaleazzo who in the family tradition was usurped by his uncle Ludovico, brother to the murdered Galeazzo. Ludovico and his wife Beatrice patronised both arts and sciences in a brilliant and learned court until Milan was taken by the French and Ludovico was held prisoner until his death. The duchy finally collapsed in 1535.

What motives lay behind the creation of beautiful, hand painted Tarocchi cards: self-propaganda, vanity, political ambition, affirmation of power? It has been suggested that two sets were commissioned to commemorate the wedding of Filippo and Maria and later Francesco and Bianca. A third pack might have been commissioned to mark Francesco's successfully taking the ducal crown. Who can really know why these images were commissioned? The ducal heraldic signs are much in evidence and would have been recognised by contemporaries. Between the two families 11 different sets of Tarocchi cards were begun. Of these, four sets retain only a single card. Perhaps these were no more than samples presented to a wealthy patron by a hopeful artist. We have no way of knowing. By contrast two sets are almost complete with 74 and 67 cards respectively. The 11 sets are known by the names of either the most probable artists or the owners. The Piermont-Morgan-Bergamo pack contains 74 cards. The Modrone set, named after the Visconti de Modrone, contains 67 cards. It is possible that both these sets were painted by the same artist with the exception of six cards in the Piermont deck. It was once believed that the artist was Antonio Ciognara, but it is now thought more likely that the artist was Bonifacio Bembo who was much favoured by the Visconti family.

From the playful court of Ferrara, through the violent court of Milan, Tarocchi continued on its way. It is no wonder that we find Death, The Tower, The Chariot, The Emperor, The Empress and The Fool looking back at us from these early Tarocchi sets. We take the meaning which is appropriate to the time in which we live. The Renaissance creators may well have seen a more immediate meaning in these images. Giulio Ferrario writing in 1808 puts words in the mouth of Fortuna in an imaginary dialogue. Fortuna is, of course, also The Wheel of Fortune.

Fortuna: I am that Fortuna who has made and unmade kings and
emperors. It is of no avail to worship me. Let him be aware who
sits at the top of the wheel. Let him hold fast to his treasure.

Regno: I reign at the top of the wheel as Fortune has destined me.
But if the wheel turns I may be deprived of power. Be moderate,
ye who are in power, lest you all fall to earth. Behold the honour
I am paid because I sit at the top of the wheel.

Regnavi: I reigned for a while then Fortune put me down and
deprived me of everything good. Her friendship avails not. No
friend remains when a man falls. Do not be confident when you
are rising; Fortune makes you fall with deadly blows. Hearken
to my case how I gained and lost this honour.

Regnabo: I shall reign if Fortune pleases and the wheel turns to
the fourth place. I shall be above and rule all the world. How
great is my pleasure then! Virtue moves me to speak such
words, because I plan to do justice and punish those who have
maliciously robbed the men of good estate. What joy I shall
have to be able to punish them!!

Sum Sine Regno: I am as you see without reign, down low in
wretchedness. Fortune has disclaimed me. If I should mount on
this wheel, every man would be friendly to me. Let each take
warning.

Alcune Poesie Inedite del Saviozzo et di altri autori [3]

These words might almost have been written with the Visconti-Sforzas in
mind. From their political struggles and powerful ambition came an
unexpected bonus, images of beauty which still intrigue. From the rising
and falling of these two families came something unexpected. Fortuna
truly plays her own hand which no man knows.

The esoteric history: the inner map

The true Tarot are symbols of our collective consciousness,
collated with each other so as to make spiritual sense of our
everyday experience

William G. Gray, *The Sangreal Tarot*

Though Tarocchi undeniably existed as a courtly game, we should also be aware of the cultural and spiritual currents of the time in which it was played. As we in the late twentieth century live with the vocabulary of a new age, so fifteenth-century Italy was also being awakened to what has historically been called the Renaissance, the new birth. The New Age movement of our times knows few social boundaries, but the new birth of the Renaissance was in keeping with a more restricted social order and was contained within educated and courtly circles. This was a time of great interest in Hermetic philosophy and ideas. The wisdom of the ancients beckoned then as it does now. The scholar, physician and priest Marsilio Ficino was employed by Cosimo de' Medici. In 1450 he was commissioned to translate the works of Plato. When Cosimo realised that he was approaching the end of his life, Ficino was asked to translate the Corpus Hermeticum as a priority. Ficino had a deep interest in astrology. He composed songs and hymns to each of the planets based on a symbolic harmonic structure. As we have already noted the Florentines increased the Trumps to 40 with the addition of cards representing the 12 signs of the zodiac, four elements, and the virtues, Charity, Faith, Prudence and Hope. Ficino himself was born in Florence. We should not forget the 50 cards of the Tarocchi Mantegna from 1470 which also point to the Hermetic philosophy.

Pico de Mirandola followed in the footsteps of Ficino. In addition to Latin and Greek, he knew Hebrew and thereby added Qabalah to the rich philosophical and spiritual ferment. In 1531 *De Occulta Philosophia* was published. The blend of the old and the new, the historical and the imaginative continued. Athanasius Kircher, a supreme example of Renaissance man, saw wisdom and spiritual magic in the newly emerging discoveries from Egypt. A particular bronze tablet seized the imagination. It became known as the Tablet of Isis or the Bembine tablet after a Cardinal Bembo who was related to its discovery. Its indecipherable hieroglyphs were the subject of much esoteric musing.

The associations between the Tarot and its specific use by esoteric fraternities began with the writings of Antoine Court de Gebelin, a Protestant pastor and freemason. He was a member of the Lodge of the Neuf Soeurs and the Order of the Philalèthes. Such participation points to an already existing esoteric tradition. The Order of the Philalèthes was an offshoot of the Order of the Elect Cohens which consisted of seven grades. It was based on belief in Biblical truth together with a general spiritual evolutionary scheme. Court de Gebelin was totally immersed in the metaphysics of his day. In the heightened awareness of a symbolically rich life, he was primed for personal revelation. One afternoon he happened to call on a Swiss lady, Madame la C d'H, only to find her playing a game with some friends. In this brief moment, Court de Gebelin was seized with a wild enthusiasm. He received an insight into the nature of Tarot which changed the development of Tarot itself. His revelation became the keynote of his *magnum opus*, the nine volumes of *Le Monde Primitif* in which he expounded the idea of an original golden age. Ironically we do not remember Antoine Court de Gebelin for his theory of the golden age but we do remember him for revisioning the Tarot.

His contribution has lasted into our own time. For the first time, the 22 Trumps of the Tarot and the 22 letters of the Hebrew alphabet came together. These two partners have of course never been separated since. Like many others who fell in love with the newly discovered Egyptian wonders, Court de Gebelin also fell under their magical spell. His claim for an Egyptian parentage is still deeply rooted in the group psyche. He expressed his personal revelation in *Le Monde Primitif*:

> Imagine the surprise which the discovery of an Egyptian book would cause if we learned that a work of the ancient Egyptians still existed in our time – one of the books saved from the flames which consumed their superb libraries – and which contained their purest beliefs regarding interesting things. Everyone would, no doubt, be eager to know about such a precious and extraordinary book which is already in very general use in a large part of Europe and has been in the hands of everyone for a number of centuries...

> This Egyptian book does exist. This Egyptian book is all that remains in our time of their superb libraries. It is even so common that not one scholar has condescended to bother with it since no one before us has ever suspected its illustrious origin. The book is composed of seventy-seven, even seventy-eight sheets or pictures divided into five classes, each showing things which are as varied as they are amusing and instructive. In a word this book is the game of Tarot.[4]

The influence of this Protestant pastor lives on. He recast the medieval Papess as the ancient High Priestess and the Pope as the Chief Hierophant or High Priest. Where the specific names he gave have faded, a flavour lingers on. He called the Hermit, 'The Wise Man' and the Devil, 'Typhon', identifying him as Set the enemy of Osiris. He called the Star, Sirius and the Chariot, 'Osiris Triumphant'. He renamed the World, 'Time'. Other allocations have not stood the test of time. He called the Tower, 'The Castle of Plutus' and the Hanged Man, 'Prudence'. The Last Judgement he called 'Creation' and retitled the Lovers 'Love and Marriage'. He saw the symbols of the four evangelists as the four seasons. It was Court de Gebelin who defined Tarot as the royal road, supposedly deriving this from *tar* meaning 'way' and *ro*, *ros* or *rog* meaning 'royal'. Additionally *Le Monde Primitif* included an essay by an unnamed writer, identified only as Monsieur de Comte de M. He called the Tarot, *The Book of Thoth*, a name which has also endured. Furthermore the Comte de M. emphasised the notion of Tarot as a means of fortune telling. A new chapter in the history of Tarot was about to open.

This new and heady brew of the romantic and the arcane, the historical and the allegorical, the mystical and the magical was enough to light a fire in the collective French mind. Tarot had been redefined. Fortune telling became the vogue in Paris, becoming the very thing to do. One Etteillia, whose real name was Alliette, rose to prominence on the crest of this wave. He made a 20-year successful career by reading cards, casting horoscopes, making talismans, interpreting dreams and providing instructions in magic. He created a system of Tarot cartomancy in ten volumes. He too saw an Egyptian hand at work within Tarot. He regarded the Tarot as a book of wisdom covering universal medicine, an account of creation and a history of mankind. He claimed that *The Book of Thoth* was devised by a committee of 17 magi, presided over by Hermes Trismegistus in the 171st year after the flood! Apparently, the first copy was inscribed on leaves of gold originating from a temple at Memphis. He produced the first 'rectified' Tarot pack, meaning a pack with images theoretically restored to a former arcane meaning. It was Etteillia who attributed the Fool to the number zero. This connection is still followed. However, he placed it at the end of the series, and this connection has been abandoned. In terms of fortune telling, he introduced both the significator card and the idea of reversed meaning. Both practices are followed today. He wrote extensively on numerology, alchemy, astrology and most especially on Tarot cartomancy. The vogue for cartomancy continued long after the death of Etteillia. New packs especially designed for fortune telling appeared. Fortune telling became a profession.

The writings of Gebelin and Etteillia served as a watershed. Tarot had moved into esoteric realms. Eliphas Levi, born Alphonse-Louis Constant, was to take it even further into the world of mystery and magic through a new influx of Qabalistic, Hermetic, alchemical and ancient sources. He identified the ten cards of each suit with the ten Sephiroth of the Tree of Life. He related the court cards to stages of human life and the four suits to the Tetragrammaton, the Holy Name of God. His work *Dogma de la Haute Magie* encouraged others to follow and they most certainly did. In France in 1863, a disciple of Levi's, Jean-Baptist Pitois writing under the name of Paul Christian produced *L'Homme Rouge des Tuileries*. This took the form of an old manuscript written by a monk, supposedly, and copied from 78 gold leaves from an Egyptian temple in Memphis. Christian called this the Samaritan Oracle. Its titles are as follows:

I	The Magus	XIII	The Skeleton, Reaper or Scythe
II	The Gate of the Sanctuary		
III	Isis Urania	XIV	The Two Urns or Genius of the Sun
IV	The Cubic Stone		
V	Master of the Mysteries of Arcana	XV	Typhon, The Electrical Whirlwind
VI	The Two Roads	XVI	The Beheaded or Lightning Struck Tower
VII	The Chariot of Osiris		
VIII	Themis, The Scales and the Blade	XVII	The Star of the Magi
		XVIII	Twilight
IX	The Veiled Lamp	XIX	The Resplendent Light
X	The Sphinx	XX	The Awakening of the Dead
XI	The Muzzled or Tamed Lion	0	The Crocodile
XII	The Sacrifice or the Great Work	XXI	The Crown of the Magi

In 1870 Christian published *Historie de la Magie* which contained an initiatory sequence in an Egyptian setting. What Paul Christian envisaged came to pass; Tarot was indeed to take on an initiatory function through the work of two Qabalistic orders. Both groups were founded in 1888. The Qabalistic Order of the Rosy Cross was founded in France by Marquis Stanislas de Guaita, and The Hermetic Order of the Golden Dawn was founded in England. Tarot flowered under this new impetus. In 1888 the Court de Gebelin Tarot cards were produced. In the following year, Oswald Wirth a disciple of de Guaita produced a limited edition of one hundred hand painted copies of his *Livre de Thot*. In 1889 too *The Tarot of the Bohemians* appeared, written by Gerard Encausse using the *nom de plume*, Papus. The explosion of interest in France was mirrored in England. Though it is hard to believe now, the teachings relating to the Tarot were veiled from the outside world under the cloak of the magical oath taken by every member:

> If I break this my Magical Obligation. I submit myself by my own consent to a Stream of Power set in motion by the Divine Guardians of this Order, Who live in the Light of their Perfect Justice and before Whom my Soul now stands.[5]

It was perhaps this air of secrecy which added a level of mystique that has lasted to this day. In the alchemical cauldron of the Golden Dawn a number of seminal Tarot packs were conceived. The Golden Dawn produced its own pack. This was probably a collaboration between the ideas of MacGregor Mathers and the art of his wife Moina. Mathers wrote *The Tarot its Occult Signification, Use in Fortune Telling and Method of Play*. The Rider-Waite pack was born here too in 1910 as a collaboration between Pamela Coleman-Smith and Arthur Waite. The idiosyncratic Aleister Crowley devised a unique Tarot pack with the help of the artist Lady Freida Harris. He picked up on an earlier resonance by choosing to call his pack, The Book of Thoth. The project was begun in 1938 and not completed until 1943. Freida Harris wrote of their work together.

> We tottered along for five years wrestling with the accumulated mass of tradition emanating from sources such as Freemasons, Alchemists, Rosicrucians, Kabbalists, Geometricians, Gematricians, Mathematicians, Symbolists, Philologists, Buddhists, Togas, Psychoanalysts, Astrologers even Heraldry, all of whom have left traces on the symbols employed.[6]

Paul Foster Case was an American member of the Golden Dawn who went on to found the Builders of the Adytum (BOTA). He too designed his own Tarot deck employing a modified version of the Rider-Waite imagery.

It was here in the Golden Dawn and its descendants and offshoots that the Tarot and the Tree of Life became wedded into a single magical, philosophical and spiritual system. Though Qabalah in its fullness is a separate and complex study, we can initially recognise that a relationship

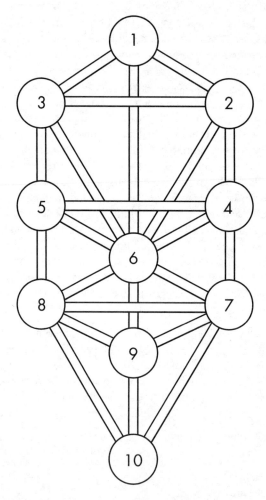

1	Kether – the Crown	6	Tiphareth – Beauty
2	Chokmah – Understanding	7	Netzach – Victory
3	Binah – Wisdom	8	Hod – Splendour
4	Chesed – Mercy	9	Yesod – the Foundation
5	Geburah – Fear	10	Malkuth – the Kingdom

Figure 1.1   The Tree of Life

between the Tarot and the Tree of Life has been forged. Although members of the Golden Dawn used Tarot for divination, their main function was primarily as a part of a ritual framework in which individual consciousness was exalted by complete immersion in a living pageant of symbolic correspondences. Sacred ritual is currently being restored and reintegrated into life. Ritual is now not uncommon whether as a solo and private devotion or as a group event. Sacred enactment, meditation and focused awareness is now seen in a positive light as an agency for healing, self-development and personal growth. At the turn of the century it smacked only of the occult, the bizarre and the dangerous. Straddling the borderland between Victorian and Edwardian restraints, the vision of the Golden Dawn was bold, adventurous and utterly extraordinary. Its members looked to Egyptian, alchemical, Hermetic and Qabalistic images for soul nourishment in preference to a stultified contemporary morality. We cannot afford to ignore the contribution of the Golden Dawn if we are to understand the roots of Tarot which are now deeply embedded in group consciousness. So we will begin with the simplest presentation of the Tree of Life. It has 22 Paths, ten emanations (the Sephiroth) and four worlds. The Tarot has 22 Triumphs, 10 numbered cards and four court cards in each suit. We can already begin to see how these two systems might profitably be merged.

As we proceed we will explore the relationship between the Tarot and the Tree of Life a little more deeply. Tarot has come a long way from Tarocchi. We should not be disconcerted by its adaptability. Contemporary Tarot is still evolving and as we move into areas of cyberspace and virtual reality, Tarot will no doubt continue to provide the hooks upon which we may place ideas, belief, concepts and values.

MacGregor Mathers like his predecessor, Court de Gebelin, played a few word games of his own and gave us the following:

Tora: Law, Hebrew
Troa: Gate, Hebrew
Rota: Wheel, Latin
Orat: It speaks, argues or entreats, Latin
Taor or Taur: Egyptian Goddess of darkness
Athor or Hathor: Egyptian Goddess of joy

The less well known Nancy Fulwood writing in 1929 also played word games when she suggested seven ways of Tarot:

Pano Tarot: Pure Spiritual Mind
Fano Tarot: The Force of the Heart
Tano Tarot: The Force of Universal Wealth
Sano Tarot: The Force of Inspiration
Rano Tarot: The Force of Faith
Ono Tarot: The Force of Hope
Gano Tarot: The Force of Universal Love

So let us close this introductory overview with these thoughts: hope, faith, inspiration, universal wealth, universal love, pure spiritual mind, the force of the heart. Perhaps you will find all of these and more besides.

2 APPROACHING THE TAROT

It is important to work and take pains, to be purposeful. When one enters the field of the Tarot, work is essential, for without work it will give you nothing.

Oswald Wirth, *Introduction to the Study of Tarot*

Welcome to the Tarot

We now move from the past into the present. Today people come to the Tarot as a metaphysical tool not as a courtly game. The esoteric associations have become too firmly interwoven for the Tarot to return to an exoteric pastime. Though we think of Tarot primarily in terms of a reading, there is far more to Tarot than this. Tarot is now used as a tool for reflection, self-awareness and creative personal development. Its images have therapeutic value. Its images have creative value. Tarot is a book of life. Tarot is a book of wisdom. As you meet the Tarot, you meet yourself.

If you are already familiar with the Tarot you will have no need for an introduction. If Tarot is a new area for you take the Tarot pack that you are going to work with and spread it out. You will find 78 cards. Spend time looking at the images. Just immerse yourself in the style, colour and richness of the Tarot as pictures. Finally, divide the pack into groups that make sense to you. You will find characters, courtly figures and the numbered cards of four suits which are not unlike the more familiar playing cards. Welcome to the Tarot.

As you set out to approach the Tarot you already bring all your previous experiences to the subject. Your own experiences will influence your expectations and needs. So as we jointly set out to approach the Tarot, let us begin at the only meaningful starting point, namely you. The following seed thoughts are for your use. Each seed thought can help you see where you stand today in relation to the Tarot. You can use the questions in any way that you find helpful. You can begin a Tarot journal with these questions if you wish. Although diary keeping requires time and commitment, it provides a personal record for the future so you may feel it is worth making the effort from the start.

THOUGHTS ON TAROT

You have expressed an interest in teaching yourself Tarot. How and why have you arrived at this decision/feeling/intention?

What do you already know/believe about Tarot?

What have been the major formative influences in your life journey so far? –
psychological/transpersonal/humanistic/magical/esoteric/spiritual/religious/historical/feminist/New Age?

How does Tarot fit with your religious/spiritual upbringing?

The Fool sets out on a new journey

At this point in your life, what do you think you want from Tarot? For example:

- ■ To be able to use Tarot as a method of divination.
- ■ To gain a deeper insight into yourself.
- ■ To deepen your understanding of symbols.
- ■ To develop your intuition.
- ■ To develop your creativity.
- ■ To deepen your meditative and spiritual life.

What expectations do you have about this book?

When you have completed your answers, find the card of The Fool and look at the image.

Like the Fool, you are about to undertake a journey. See that the character is about to take a great leap. See that the Fool carries a knapsack. Your knapsack is invisible to the outside world but you carry it all the same. It contains all the experiences, memories, attitudes, values and beliefs that you have acquired up to this moment. The Fool is about to take a significant step over an abyss into a new realm. If you are coming to the Tarot for the first time you are about to do the same. If you are already familiar with the Tarot you have already taken this step in your life. The Fool is a card of beginnings and new adventures. A new study brings a new adventure and a new beginning.

Taking a leap into the unknown

Before looking at the Tarot in more detail, let us first look at the process of learning something new. Whenever we tackle a new project, initially we sense our own lack of familiarity with the material and the language of the subject. We become consciously aware of the mental struggle to remember and reproduce what we are trying to learn. Constant exposure to the subject brings familiarity and we begin to feel at ease with the concepts and vocabulary of the project. This move from the unfamiliar to the familiar takes time as learning becomes integrated. Eventually the struggle is past and the new learning is integrated, the subject is no longer new but familiar. Learning about the Tarot is no different.

We can define our approach to the Tarot in three phases or stages. If the Tarot is totally new for you, then you will recognise the needs of the first stage. If you already have some familiarity with the Tarot, then your main emphasis will be on the needs expressed through the second and third stages.

Stage 1: Getting intellectual information through analysis

Stage 1 involves using the intellect, that is, the left side of the brain. It is the application of memory and conscious learning skills. In relation to teaching yourself the Tarot the following steps will occur:

1 You will learn to recognise and identify the structure of the Tarot, which is divided up as follows:

■ The Major Arcana, comprising the 22 Trumps.
■ The Minor Arcana, comprising the rest of the cards in the Four Suits which are commonly depicted as:

– Discs, or Coins,
– Swords,
– Rods, Batons and Wands,
– Cups.

2 You will begin to recognise and identify the symbolism of the Tarot and to categorise these meaningfully.

Stage 2: Opening intuitive understanding through synthesis

Stage 2 involves using the intuition, that is, using the right side of the brain. This is the development of insight and inner awareness. In relation to teaching yourself the Tarot, the following steps will occur:

1 You will establish a relationship with the 22 Archetypal characters of the Major Arcana.
2 You will establish a relationship with the Tarot Courts and the Elemental Paths of the Minor Arcana.
3 You will internalise symbols of the Tarot through meditation and exploration.

Stage 3: Living by wisdom as gnosis

Stage 3 involves accessing higher consciousness through the birth of transcendent understanding. In relation to teaching yourself the Tarot, the following steps will occur:

1 You will find self-realisation and self-knowledge.
2 You will find the reflecting mirror of the Major Arcana and the Minor Arcana.

Teach yourself Tarot

Teaching and learning are two sides of the same coin. There is always a dynamic flow between the teacher and the student. In this case, you have come to learn Tarot but the Tarot will also be your teacher. You have already permitted The Fool to show you a reflection of yourself as a beginner on a new journey. Other Tarot figures will also reveal new reflections for you as the journey progresses. Teaching and learning are familiar words and concepts for us all, yet neither quite explains the depth and fullness of our approach to the Tarot. It is clear that both teaching and learning will take place but ultimately these prove to be just pathways to the third stage which we have called gnosis. Learning about the Tarot through study and teaching yourself through application, are in fact preparatory processes for entry into the reflecting mirror which is Tarot. This third stage is perhaps the most difficult to explain or describe. You will recognise this threshold when you reach it for it is at this point that the Tarot realm naturally opens up as a source of creativity and inspiration.

The three stages outlined in our approach are not hard and fast divisions. There is much interaction between the first and second stages, the intellectual and intuitive approaches. These can be regarded as complementary ways of learning. The third stage, like the top floor of a skyscraper, cannot arise except through the firm foundations of intellectual grasp and intuitive vision. Intellectual study clearly has its place as the Tarot makes frequent connection with other areas of study such as mythology, psychology and astrology. If these areas currently mean little to you, then you have plenty of scope for reading and research of your own. It is a mistake to come to the Tarot as a retreat for the intuition. If you miss the point of a mythological allusion, for example, your intuition will also miss the mark. If you do not recognise a symbol, you cannot interpret it. So come to the Tarot with your intellect and your intuition but most of all come prepared to interact. This is not a work book but it does ask you to engage with the work of Tarot which is also the Great Work. If you engage willingly with the Tarot it will repay you handsomely. Begin with analysis, seek synthesis, incubate gnosis.

Analysis is the process of dividing the whole into parts to make observation simpler. In fact Tarot shows you the instrument of analysis which is the sword of the mind. What kind of sword is in your keeping? Is it sharp and bright or rusty and pitted? Does it pull easily from the scabbard from regular use, or perhaps both sword and scabbard have been long buried? Find the card, the Ace of Swords and look at it. Here is the sword of the mind ready to dissect with decisive stroke and keen edge. See that the sword is held in a firm grip; mind and body work together as one. A crown bearing vegetation is magically suspended at the sword's point. The sword of the mind will make its point. In debate or reasoned argument, nothing is worse than missing the point but this blade will strike home. Will you do the same? See how easily we have moved from one mode to the other. Holding the image of the bright sword will sharpen your mental faculties and analytical abilities. Intuition strengthens the intellect by adding another dimension of understanding.

Integrating intellectual information is a familiar process but the development of a reliable intuition represents a leap into unknown territory. Let us employ an analogy to compare the intellectual and intuitive functions. The intellectual mind is like a bag which contains facts. It only holds the facts that have been consciously placed within it. Memory is the main tool for locating what is in the bag but sometimes the facts that you want to recall are hard to find. The intellectual mind stores only what has been given. A fact is either found or not. The intuition by contrast is like a living tree within the mind. It is planted with a seed-thought and nurtured through classical techniques of visualisation, reflection, meditation and recollection. These techniques permit the concentrated examination of a single thought or constellation of thoughts. The seed takes root and inner growth takes place through an expansion of understanding and awareness. The intuition tree sends out many branches and makes its own connection with other seeds likewise growing in the mind. Every symbol is a seed. The unlimited associations of symbolic thought feed the imagination and open the mind. The more seeds which take firm root in the mind, the richer the harvest will be. The intuition is capable of understanding above and beyond its original seed-thought. The intuition does not depend on memory but on realisation. There is much to be gained from developing the intuition in addition to the intellectual powers of reason, deduction and judgement. It brings an additional dimension to perception, not merely in relation to the study of Tarot but to life itself.

Many people have little sense of the intuitive. It seems to represent all that is erratic, irrational and even fearful. Robert Assagioli, the founder of Psychosynthesis, remarks that, 'Intuition is one of the least recognised and least appreciated and therefore one of the repressed or underdeveloped functions.'[1] So let us prepare ourselves for that leap into that less familiar territory. Developing intuition is a gentle and organic process of awakening the function of insight, which is the power of inner sight. It is the awakened eye of the mind. It is the active power of inner vision. Let us first think of intuition as your inner tuition. In other words it is an expression of what you really understand in the moment. It is not a repeated phrase from childhood conditioning. It is not a parroted refrain nor an easy platitude. It is not a fragment of handed down dogma or a glib reply but your unique and full response to any given situation. The intuition is close to the instinctive gut response. It is the expression of body wisdom and heart knowing. The intuition cannot function in competition with the analytical drive of the intellect. Only when the intellect is quietened, even temporarily through meditative practices, can the small voice of the intuition be heard.

As a society we place little or no value on the intuition. Conversely Assagioli places much value on the development of the intuition:

> Those most in need of its compensating power are over intellectualised people.[2]

Assagioli even considers that without the development of intuitive skills, we remain incomplete:

> The purpose of activating the intuition is that of putting at the disposal of the individual a precious function which generally remains latent and underused therefore leaving the individual incomplete in his or her own development.[3]

This is a powerful statement. Society at large places much value on intellectual development and little value on intuitive ability. The positive contribution of the intuitive sense has been disregarded at a high price. The honed intuition is not hit-and-miss guesswork but a reliable and accurate measure. It is neither eccentric nor emotionally based but a crystal clear and lucid inner knowing. It should not be confused with the psychic skills such as clairaudience and clairvoyance or precognition. Inner tuition functions through conscious and full awareness of the dynamics of the present moment. Intuition is not a substitute for reason but an adjunct to it. Your inner relationship with the Tarot will serve to develop your intuition. Visualisation, meditation and contemplation are holistic ways of learning. So be confident that you can learn through your own inner tuition. Deep and sustained insight opens the door to consciousness of an altogether different order, namely the consciousness which is living wisdom. The Tarot is often referred to as a book of Ancient or Perennial Wisdom. Contemplate for a moment if you will, the nature of wisdom. Here is an uncommon quality. We have moved into the province of sages and teachers, the spiritually awakened and the fully conscious. But we should not make the mistake of believing that wisdom belongs only to the great, the good and the holy. Assagioli points us to a realm of being beyond the common. It may be uncommon but it remains within reach:

> The basic premise or hypothesis is that there exists in addition to those parts of the unconscious we have called the lower and middle unconscious, including the collective unconscious, another vast realm of our inner being which has for the most part been neglected.[4]

Spiritual traditions have developed ways and means into this realm. The mystical and the universal open us to the transcendent realm of wisdom. In Assagioli's psychological/spiritual system it is the transcendent symbol which takes us towards this realm. This statement is a powerful affirmation of the significance of Tarot. The Tarot is a symbol system brimming with transcendent symbols. We have placed considerable value on the Tarot, now let us make our first sustained approach.

Encountering the Major Arcana

> We might do well to meditate on these personages and ask ourselves if there is not something of each of them in us.
>
> Oswald Wirth, *Introduction to the Study of the Tarot*

As we have already seen the cards of the Major Arcana are known as Trumps, a term derived from the Italian *trionfi* meaning triumphs. The term *Arcana* is derived from the Latin *arcanum* meaning a mystery or a secret. The Trumps of the Major Arcana consist of 22 cards. We will come to the Major Arcana not as a lifeless list but as a living carnival of characters. Let us use the Renaissance background of the Tarot as our first introduction to the characters of the Tarot pageant. In this way we can satisfy both intellectual and intuitive demands at one time. As we meet the Tarot characters in the interior world of consciousness, we have the opportunity firstly to learn their names and secondly to become acquainted through engaging in an imaginary scenario. This approach is far more effective than relying purely on memory skills. It will, however, strengthen remembrance.

The visualisation is long, so feel free to divide it into as many segments as you can cope with at one time. If visualisation is a new skill, then perhaps just encounter one character at a time. Though it will be helpful if you have each of the Trumps in front of you as you proceed, not all of the visualisations may accord entirely with the imagery of your card set. At the end of your meditation write down anything that springs to mind. Always remember that your own thoughts and realisations are what matter. You can use the meditation in any way that suits your needs. The classic masque belonged to this world of romance, chivalry and intrigue. So let us meet the Tarot characters in this setting. In keeping with the original term, *carte da trionfi*, we will refer to the characters as Triumphs rather than Trumps.

The Carnival Pageant

> A favourite entertainment in the courts of Renaissance Italy was the staging of just such triumphal processions, with floats bearing figures derived from mythology or representing abstractions such as Love and Death.
>
> Michael Dummett, *The Game of Tarot*

Imagine that you have been invited to a festival. In accordance with the custom of the times you find yourself wearing a costume of your choice. You also find yourself standing on the spacious balcony of a comfortable Italian house in a city square. In the streets below crowds have already gathered to watch the parade. You will have a first class view. A trumpet sounds and you hear the approaching rumble of heavy wheels on cobbled stones. The parade is close. A roar goes up from the crowd and the parade enters the square amid much noise and wild cheering. From your vantage point, you can see everything.

The Triumph of the Fool

The first float comes into view. It is decorated with a mountain landscape set against a brilliant yellow sky. You see nothing here but empty space. Everyone watches the space in anticipation. Unexpectedly a door opens in the yellow of the sky and a figure steps through accompanied by a small dog which now yaps at his feet. He carries his belongings in a small pouch at the end of a stick which is balanced over one shoulder. In the other hand he carries a white rose. This figure wears a decorated costume of the courtly fool. He extends the white rose towards the assembly and a delicate scent is carried on the breeze. In a moment he has passed out of sight.

The Triumph of the Magician

Next comes the float bearing the figure of the Magician. He stands behind a table set with a cup, a sword, a pentacle (a disc inscribed by a five-pointed star) and a rod. With great inner composure he raises each in turn. He raises a dignified salute with the sword. Next he upholds the cup. Then he raises the pentacle. Finally he extends the rod towards the assembly. These simple ceremonial gestures seem like the opening sequence of a theatrical drama. As you reflect on this, the next float appears in view.

The Triumph of the High Priestess

This is the float bearing the figure of the High Priestess. A woman is seated upon a throne which stands between two columns. A gauzy veil hangs between them. In her lap she holds an open book. The crowd falls quiet with an expectant hush but she does not speak. She sits perfectly still as she passes by, yet you feel that she sees into everything. Her eyes meet yours momentarily and you feel as if she has seen deeply into your being. She passes and her spell is broken.

The Triumph of the Empress

Next comes the float bearing the Empress. She is seated on a throne set in outdoor landscape among wheat and flowers. She is crowned and holds an upraised sceptre. Her robe is embroidered with pomegranates. The crowd cheers in warm response to her presence. She throws handfuls of wheat to the crowd. Everyone wants this largesse which is the gift of the earth. She beams a great smile. Her presence is stately yet powerful. She exudes a natural and easy warmth. Her presence brings a warmth to your heart. Now she too is gone.

The Triumph of the Emperor

Next the Emperor comes into view. He is seated on a throne decorated with ram's heads. He wears the helmet and armour of a man of action. His body looks strong. He is armed and looks ready to spring to your defence in any situation. His presence inspires total confidence. He too holds a sceptre. The crowd roars its approval as he passes on his way. He raises his sceptre to receive the approbation of the assembly. The cheering dies away only slowly as he passes from view.

The Triumph of the Hierophant

In total contrast next comes the float bearing the Hierophant. The crowd falls quiet once more and many respectfully lower their heads. Here is a priestly figure in the vestments and regalia of the spiritual life. He wears three colours, red, white and blue. His outer robe is marked with three crosses and he bears a crown of three tiers. He carries a staff topped with three bars. He sits upon a throne set on a raised dais which is decorated by crossed keys. He is seated between two columns. As he passes through the crowd, he extends a blessing with a traditional gesture.

The Triumph of the Lovers

The next float carries two figures. You cannot help thinking of the Garden of Eden for here you see the apple tree and the serpent. Yet you also see the bush which does not burn. Here stand Adam and Eve, Everyman and Everywoman. Here are two young lovers ready to launch themselves into life's journey. In the background you see the image of a path and mountain which lie ahead of them. The figure of an angel is also depicted here. You feel that an unseen blessing is being bestowed, for the angel reaches out over the pair with outstretched hands.

The Triumph of the Chariot

The next float bears the figure of a man standing in a decorated chariot pulled by two sphinxes of black and white. He has the bearing of the victor upon him. He exudes self-confidence, prowess and natural authority. He is charismatic and radiates life and vigour. All the attention of the crowd falls upon him. A roar of approval goes up from the assembly with a single voice. He is the people's hero. He is the Charioteer. Too soon he is gone and the crowd subsides once more.

The Triumph of Strength

The next float comes into view and reveals a startling scene. A woman stands dressed simply in white. A garland of flowers extends from one shoulder and is wrapped around a lion which stands beside her. The woman and the lion are united by nothing more than a garland of roses. She strokes its head. The crowd instinctively backs away. The lion licks her hand. You feel amazement and wonder at the scene, but you also feel a sense of relief as she passes from view and takes danger with her.

The Triumph of the Hermit

Next comes a float bearing an old man clad in dark robes. He is the Hermit. He seems so ancient. You briefly catch sight of his face which conveys the wisdom of the ages. There is something unworldly about him. You sense a deep renunciation of worldly trappings. You feel that he carries all his possessions with him as he travels alone. A lantern is held out before him as he walks on unaccompanied. He holds up the lantern and views the crowd. He has no need of anything. He just pulls his cloak around his head as the float continues on its way.

The Triumph of the Wheel of Fortune

The next float rumbles into view. It carries a huge contraption in the form of a wheel. You hear the sound of ancient wood, grinding and creaking as it turns. At its centre is a hub inscribed with a complicated symbol. Around the rim you see the letters 't', 'o', 'r' and 'a'. As the wheel moves you realise that these same letters also spell 'rota' which means wheel. At the top of the wheel sits a sphinx armed with a sword. Tied to the outside of the wheel is a strange creature with a human body and animal head. As the wheel moves so it too is moved just a little closer towards the sphinx. You wonder when the sphinx and creature might meet.

The Triumph of Justice

The next float arrives bearing the seated figure of the judiciary. An upraised sword is held in one hand, the scales of justice hang in the other. You find yourself contemplating this most abstract quality. What deeds and circumstances might be placed in the scales to ascertain justice? The Egyptians weighed the deeds of the heart against the feather of truth. How will your heart weigh in the balance?

The Triumph of the Hanged Man

The next float bears a strange sight indeed. It carries a hanging tree and a figure of a young man hangs suspended here. This figure carries none of the terror of the common criminal so often publicly executed in such squares before crowds. This face shows only serenity and peace. The complete contradiction between mind and body seems overwhelming. As the figure passes from view all you remember is his gentle smile.

The Triumph of Death

Now here comes the float bearing the figure of Death. Everyone instinctively looks away, for everyone knows death as plague, pestilence and war. This figure is robed and hooded. You cannot see his face, for death has many faces. He carries the traditional scythe and its sharp edge glints in the light. As he passes from view everyone breathes a collective sigh of relief. Death is familiar enough already.

The Triumph of Temperance

By contrast to the sombre and dark now here comes a figure radiating life and light. Dressed in white, this figure smiles deeply from within. In the semblance of an angel, Temperance stands before you. In one hand Temperance holds a silver chalice and in the other a chalice of gold. Like a magician performing to thrill an audience Temperance pours the contents from one to another with great flourish. As you watch, it seems that some true magic is taking place for as the contents flow from one to the other not a drop is spilled and neither chalice ever overflows.

The Triumph of the Devil

Now comes a strange sight. A hybrid figure is seated on a block of stone. The head is misshapen and carries two horns. The upper body appears to be human but leathery wings emerge from the back. The legs are animal-like and end in claws. The crowd falls silent. Everyone averts their eyes lest they catch his gaze. Now the silence is broken as he lets out a mocking laugh. Why is he laughing at you all?

The Triumph of the Tower

Now comes a scene of chaos and destruction. A building is burning, its fallen bricks litter the ground. In its own historical context, the destroyed tower has a grim and common reality. To add to the illusion, you hear the theatrical sounds of thunder off stage. Lightning crackles with dramatic effect. You remember the destructive power of the storm. It is a relief when the scene of chaos passes and you are left thinking of the work required for reconstruction.

The Triumph of the Star

A float now comes into view. It is painted entirely as the heavens. All is dark blue studded with tiny pin pricks of brilliance. You see only the representation of the starry sky. There seems to be no figure to greet you here. Yet even as you look, you see a movement. A woman painted just as the background steps forwards. She is dressed in a close fitting costume of dark blue spangled with stars. She lifts up a single star and elevates it like an offering. Finally she steps back and merges with the background as she is camouflaged against the heavens.

The Triumph of the Moon

Here comes the next float. An eerie pale light fills the scene. In the foreground is a shallow pool. A woman in a silver robe stands before you. With a sweeping gesture of her arm, she draws your attention to the background where you see a luminous moon-face set overlooking a path. Moonlight is reflected on the surface of the water. Many stories tell of attempts to catch the light of the Moon. The woman in silver kneels beside the pool and scoops up moon-water. The reflection settles. The Moon is in the sky and in the water. Her hands are now empty.

The Triumph of the Sun

Here comes the float of the Sun. It is painted with a brilliant blue sky which is decorated by a huge sun-face. Before it stands a young man in golden armour which catches the sunlight and reflects it back to the ground with every small movement he makes. He is dazzling and radiant. As the light bounces from his armour people shield their eyes. He looks glorious.

The Triumph of Judgement

A figure dressed as an angel raises a trumpet to his lips. As the horn is sounded a deep resonance reverberates throughout the crowd. The sound ripples through you like a wave. There is magic in sound. Here is a wake-up call straight from the heavens. Who could ignore such a sound? The trumpet is sounded once more and you feel your whole being quake. You look around you and notice that while some of the crowd are fixed to the spot by the sound others chatter in little groups as if nothing had happened.

The Triumph of the World

Now the last float comes into view. A figure swathed in purple kneels within an oval wreath of laurel which fills the scene. The figure rises and begins to dance. All eyes are upon her. As she dances she sets up a sounded note which is taken up by the crowd. A vibration embraces dancer and assembly. The dancer holds a tipped wand in each hand and with each step, trails of light seem to radiate and hang briefly in the air as spirals of brilliance. The assembly watch mesmerised with a feeling of awe. Finally her dance is finished, the sound dies away. The dancer returns to her kneeling position. The crowd spontaneously does the same. There is a great feeling of blessing. She passes from view.

Now characters dressed in carnival costume move among the crowd distributing scrolls. You receive yours and unroll the parchment. It contains all the names of the characters in the pageant, it is yours to keep: the Fool – the Magician – the High Priestess – the Empress – the Emperor – the Hierophant – the Lovers – the Chariot – Strength – the Hermit – the Wheel of Fortune – Justice – the Hanged Man – Death – Temperance – the Devil – the Tower – the Star – the Moon – the Sun – Judgement – the World.

You have now encountered the characters of the Major Arcana in a brief but personal way. Your diary should now contain your comments and thoughts. First impressions always count but we will meet each of the characters again.

Encountering the Minor Arcana

When you wish to proceed with your inner exploration, we will journey to encounter the dynamics of the elemental powers expressed through the Minor Arcana. Who better to teach us than the Magician himself? We can combine our need for intellectual information with our desire to develop our own intuitive skills. You might like to record the journey on tape, or read it slowly aloud several times so that all the details sink in before actually closing your eyes and re-creating the sequence in your mind. If you are exploring the Tarot in a group, one person might lead the journey for the others.

THE MAGICIAN'S TABLE

Have the Tarot Trump I in front of you and make sure that you are familiar with all its details. In other words ensure that you can re-create the image in your mind's eye. When you are ready, enter your own state of meditation and call the full image to mind within the frame of the card. In your mind's eye allow the frame to expand and become as an open doorway. Now see the figure of the Magician as if he were standing at his table just beyond the doorway. See yourself walking through the doorway until you stand before the table of the Magician. Here you see the cup and rod, sword and pentacle. Deepen your own state of meditation. Become aware of the gentle perfume of roses and lilies which hangs in the air. The Magician is involved in his own meditation. He stands with one arm raised aloft, the other points down to the earth. In his upraised hand a wand seems to shine in the light. He sees you and drops the upraised arm placing the wand on the table. His eyes meet yours. He seems to read your mind and know your purpose.

Meet the Magician of the Tarot

He now reaches towards the table and with great reverence picks up the chalice in both hands. He extends it towards you and you step forward. He offers you his communion. You drink. As you do so, you hear the words: 'Drink deep, here are the waters of life. Honour your own feelings and those of others. Acknowledge your own feelings and those of others. Contemplate the life of the emotions.' Enter more deeply into your own awareness and contemplate your own emotional life. Maintain this awareness for as long as you need. Return the chalice to the Magician who places it back on the table.

Now he lifts the rod from the table with both hands and comes to stand before you; he extends his arms and offers you the rod with utter gentleness. You take it from him and hold it in your two hands. It seems only natural to uplift it towards the heavens in a gesture of reverence. As you do so, momentarily the rod seems to radiate an inner light of its own. You hear the words: 'Raise up that which comes from the great above. Acknowledge that which lies at the core of your being. Honour your own inner tuition which is the fire of the spirit. Honour this spark in others. Contemplate your own inner tuition.' Enter more deeply into your own awareness and contemplate your own intuitive life. Maintain this awareness for as long as you need. When you are ready hand the rod back to the Magician who returns it to the table.

Now he lifts the sword from the table and coming to stand before you he raises it aloft in a gesture of salutation. He lowers the sword and hands it to you. You repeat his gesture lifting the sword above your head. You hear the words: 'Proclaim the powers of the mind. Honour the mind which is as invisible as the air you breathe. Honour the mind in others and you will come to find the universal mind which supports all.' Enter more deeply into your own awareness and contemplate your own mental state. What thoughts normally fill your mind and occupy your interest? Maintain this awareness for as long as you need. When you are ready hand the sword back to the Magician who returns it to the table.

Next he lifts the pentacle from the table. He holds it up to the heavens and then comes to you and places it in your hands. You see a disc inscribed by a star with five points. As you gaze upon it you hear the words: 'See the circle of the earth inscribed by the five-pointed star. Stretch your limbs and you will find that you are the star at the centre of the circle. Here is the physical world of the four elements vivified by the fifth power of akasa. See matter and spirit united in yourself, see it united in others, see it united everywhere.' Contemplate this unity. Enter more deeply into your own awareness and contemplate the unity of spirit and matter. Maintain this awareness for as long as you need. When you are ready hand the pentacle back to the Magician who returns it to the table.

Finally the Magician speaks directly to you: 'Observe the table set before you. Earth, Air, Fire and Water are here together, indivisible and interdependent. Look for these same signs in the world. Look for these same powers in yourself and you will find the interdependence of all life.'

When you are ready to close the meditation, mentally step back through the doorway which you first created. Allow the scene to settle and become two-dimensional once more. Finally allow the images to dissolve and return to normal consciousness. Make any notes on your own thoughts and responses straight away before they fade.

You have now begun to interact with the Tarot. The Tarot itself is your teacher.

Summary

- You have encountered the Major Arcana.
- You have encountered the four elements of the Minor Arcana.

3 | THE WAY OF TAROT

Therefore one of the urgent needs of therapy and of education is
the realisation of the nature and power of symbols, the study of the
many classes and kinds of symbols, and their systematic utilisation
for therapeutic, educational, and self realisation purposes.

Robert Assagioli, *Psychosynthesis*

Tarot is most frequently used as a tool for divination. This is most often a
brief and commercial encounter. While keeping the function of divination
clearly in view, let us simultaneously affirm the deeper and more lasting
significance for this unique symbol system. The Tarot can be thought of as
a book without words. It is a book written in pictures. The power of the
pictorial image should come as no surprise in the day of the media image
and the computer icon. The difference between the familiar images which
surround us and the specialised images of the Tarot is that the former are
culturally bound and short-lived while the latter are universal. The images
of the Tarot are the universal symbols which speak across time. We find
the shared symbols of culture and myth: the sun and moon, the star and
rainbow: We find the traveller and the wise old man, mother nature and
the devil. We find the universal moments of birth and death, loss and love.
The Tarot speaks to us of the universal human constants in a universal
language, that of symbol. This is the way of Tarot.

These constants are often referred to as archetypes. These are the
blueprints or underlying patterns of human existence. We see them in the
Tarot and we recognise them instinctively. From recognition we pass into
interaction. Interaction elicits a response and we find ourselves moving
beneath the surface of everyday life into a more direct relationship with
the greater themes of life. This deepening of experience brings meaning
and sense of purpose. Our need for connection to the bigger themes of
universal human life is merely exaggerated by the contemporary inability
to provide such experiences. Our lives have become diminished by the

demands of the mortgage or even the dole queue. We live within the pressure of the career hothouse and the race for financial security. Technological advance enables us to communicate across the globe but do we know what is going on inside ourselves? What space is there for the vision quest? What time is there for contemplation? What place is there for ritual and communal celebration? We have lost the group ways of remembering and honouring the sacred. We become lost in the labyrinth of our own manufacture. Yet we never quite forget the faces of the great mother, or the hero, the innocent child or the woman of magic. Somewhere deep inside, we know we have to journey in order to come home. Sometimes Tarot brings the shock of recognition. Here are the faces long veiled from us, yet we recognise them as old friends for they have belonged too long to human kind to be completely forgotten. Tarot reconnects us to the greater whole at a time when we have forgotten the words of the greater language and become content to speak only in the monosyllables of a lesser language.

The way of the Tarot is the way of symbolic representation. It shows us symbol and archetypes. It asks us to move beyond the linear one-dimensional mind which cannot bring us a glimpse of the infinite and take a quantum leap towards the unlimited language of symbol, myth and metaphor. Every picture tells its own story. As you begin to think symbolically so your intuition will quicken and your ability to understand symbolic meaning will accelerate. This approach takes you into the heart of Tarot. As you understand the significance of one symbol, you will also read the same message through another guise. The Tarot is a system of symbols. It is a veritable storehouse of symbolic wealth. It is a reservoir of symbolic potency. As we proceed to become more engaged with the Tarot we need to grasp both the importance and consequences of undertaking immersion in the symbols which the Tarot has to offer us. Each symbol has the power to enrich consciousness. Words have a precision and narrow application. A symbol permits mental exploration, the unlimited association of ideas and free flow of the emotions. We think in words but develop insight through symbols. A symbol frees us from the tyranny of the mental straitjacket. It demands neither a right nor a wrong response. Instead a symbol has the power to lead the mind on an unlimited trail of associations which opens up the deeper recesses of understanding. Until we make a deeper connection to the images of the Tarot, we see only pictures. When we have internalised these same images as symbols we come into a deeper contact with a living dynamic which the symbol enshrines.

Before we move on to encounter the symbols of the Tarot, we need to understand the way in which a symbol functions for the psyche. We can perhaps understand this process through a simple analogy. Imagine an organisation administered by two offices, the front office and the back office. The front office is very small. It is staffed by a single secretary. The back office in contrast is huge and has many staff in differing capacities. It has an extensive archive which the backroom staff use constantly. The backroom staff are fully aware of all the actions taken by the secretary in the front office. However, the communication system between the two offices is far from ideal. Instructions, notes and other transactions are transmitted only through a small window and most often are written in brief and cryptic code. The secretary never meets the staff of the back office directly and communications arrive without explanation. The problems between the two offices are not difficult to predict, the solution also appears obvious to an outsider. Better communication would serve both offices equally. Yet moving away from the analogy it is painfully evident that consciousness and the unconscious, which both so need a mutual language, also seem blighted not to find it. The powers of the conscious mind are highly prized by our Western culture. We are inculcated into the functions of the front office secretary from an early age. Education especially serves as a tool for developing and refining the powers of deduction, rationality and mental precision. Unbalanced development is far from healthy and serves only to repress the unconscious and create a potential for dynamic explosion. As Jung says:

> Civilised life today demands concentrated, directed conscious functioning and this entails the risk of considerable disassociation from the unconscious.[1]

One function is over developed so often at the expense of the other. Jung saw that a balance between these two could be held by the appearance of an intermediary which he called the transcendent function. We can understand its purpose through the analogy of the two offices both sorely in need of a shared language. The transcendent function or third party must be neutral, yet must serve both interests. It must be understood by both parties and must be able to reveal the needs of the one to the other. As a mediator serves to unblock the stalemate between two warring camps so the transcendent function, the third party, serves the interests of both and permits a new exchange to take place. The symbolic language which is Tarot stands ready to function in the capacity of mediator between conscious understanding and unconscious need. As the third party brings peace to a dispute, the transcendent symbol eases inner tension by making inner peace. The Tarot offers us a rich storehouse of transcendent symbols. As we incorporate these images, we expand and extend our own symbolic repertoire. In effect we provide the unconscious with a readily available language.

Psychological theory can seem removed from the circumstances of ordinary life. David Whyte, a contemporary poet, speaks simply of this same process:

> The summoning of internal imagery may seem like the description of miraculous oracular powers but it is really a simple process of uncovering something our deeper psyche already knows. The deep psyche, or soul left to find its way, will offer up or recognise in the outer world images germane to its place on the path of life. That's it, the soul seems to say, that's how it looks from here, that's it.[2]

The soul speaks through internal imagery. So let's equip it with a rich voice.

Symbols: the seeds for growth

> Symbolic language is a language in its own right, in fact the only universal language the human race ever developed.
>
> Eric Fromm, *The Forgotten Language*

Significant developments in the field of humanistic psychology provide important insights into the value of Tarot as a symbol system. Psychosynthesis, the system devised by Robert Assagioli, is built upon the presentation of symbolic material in a therapeutic setting. He tells us exactly how we might approach any given symbol:

> Symbols can be visualised and this sets into motion unconscious psychological processes. This is an effective means for the transformation of the unconscious.[3]

This is more than a clue, it is a working tool which we may take and make our own. Jung knew this too and referred to it as the creative imagination.

The terminology is not important, the practical reality of the experience alone counts. Visualisation is a practical experience. It is quite unlike thinking about something. It is different because it draws upon different parts of the brain. Descriptive language remains a function of the left hemisphere, the creation of images belongs to the right hemisphere. The former lacks the emotional intensity of a personal response, the latter lacks the objectivity of intellectual rigour. The two functions together yield a rich harvest of ideas and inspiration.

Visualising images in the mind's eye is something of a forgotten art in days of so much external imagery. The television and cinema have done much to dampen the imaginative powers of the mind. If you wish to discover or perhaps rediscover this faculty for yourself, you only need to make the effort to close your physical eyes and open the eye of the mind. This ability is often sluggish but will sharpen with practice and use. The creative imagination is responsive to descriptive language and also to memory. If you have seen a rose, you can draw upon memory to re-create it. If you have rested in a cornfield on a summer afternoon you can re-create it. If you have dipped your fingers into flowing water, you can re-create the sensation. People differ in their ability to re-create these internal scenarios. Although more people respond best to visual description, others find it easier to re-create internal imagery using auditory clues while still others use kinaesthetic and even olfactory clues. In other words when you are attempting to re-create an internal scene give your mind the fullest range of sensory stimuli possible by offering yourself rich description. Include any sounds related to the scene and provide the opportunity for touching and even making contact with your imaginary world through the evocation of scents, perfumes and aromas.

To repeat Assagioli's words once more for emphasis, 'Symbols can be visualised and this sets into motion unconscious psychological processes. This is an effective means for the transformation of the unconscious.' The central significance of this statement cannot be emphasised enough. It holds the key to the potential within your personal interaction with the Tarot.

Visualisation of Symbol → Sets in Motion → Process of Transformation

There is no value in visualising an image for its own sake. It is rather a means of active exploration. Like laying down a fishing line we are casting into deep waters and waiting for a catch. It is this relationship between casting and catching, creating images within the mind and reaping the results in the total psyche which facilitates personal growth and change. It is this living process which lies at the heart of interaction with the Tarot. If we accept the significance of symbolic material we can approach the Tarot with a degree of respect and admiration. If we affirm what Assagioli states, namely that it is possible 'to utilise the enormous and by far not yet realised potency of symbols of psychological life',[4] then we may rediscover the Tarot in the spirit of this same quest. Not only does Assagioli affirm the importance of the symbol and present us with the practical tools for undertaking this process but he presents us with the particular symbols which he considered to be powerful as agents of personal transformation. He presents us with seven categories of significant symbols. As we examine these symbols we will find that they form the language of Tarot itself. If we do not recognise every single symbol in one Tarot pack, we will surely find them as we explore the vast number of Tarot sets now available.

Seven categories of transcendent symbolism

The seven categories of transcendent symbolism, with some examples, are as follows:

1 **Natural symbols**: Earth, air, fire, water, sky, stars, Sun, Moon, mountain, sea, stream, river, lake, pond, wind, cloud, fog, tree, cave, flame, wheat, seed, flowers, rose, lotus, sunflower, jewels, light (sunrise, rays of light, darkness).

2 **Animal symbols**: lion, tiger, bear, snake, wolf, deer, bull, goat, worm, chrysalis-butterfly, birds, domestic animals, the egg.

3 **Human symbols**: father, mother, grandfather, grandmother, son, daughter, sister, brother, child, wise old man, magician, king, queen, prince, princess, knight, teacher, the human heart, the human hand, the eye, birth, growth, death and resurrection.

4 **Man-made symbols**: bridge, channel, reservoir, tunnel, flag, fountain, lighthouse, candle, road, path, wall, door, house, castle, stairway, ladder, mirror, box, sword.

5 **Religious symbols: Western**: God, the Christ, holy mother, angels, devils, saints or holy men, priest, monk, nun, resurrection, hell, purgatory, heaven, the grail, temple, chapel, cross. **Eastern**: Brahma, Vishnu, Shiva, the Buddha. **Mythological symbols**: pagan gods and goddesses, heroes, Apollo, the Muses, the Three Graces, Venus, Diana, Orpheus, Hercules, Vulcan, Pluto, Saturn, Mars, Mercury, Jupiter, Wotan, Seigfreid, Brunhilda, Valhalla, the Nibelungen, the Valkyries.

6 **Teacher**: wise man, old man, magician.

7 **Abstract symbols: Numbers**: as Pythagorean symbols. **Geometrical**: dot, cross, equilateral triangle, square, diamond, stars – five pointed and six pointed etc. **Three-dimensional figures**: sphere, cube, cone, ascending spiral.

Let us look for Assagioli's seven categories in the Tarot. This is an investigation which you can pursue for yourself using your own Tarot pack. Even a brief examination will show you that the symbols presented through the Tarot correlate extremely closely to the symbols valued by Psychosynthesis. This relationship should enable us to define Tarot as a working tool of personal and spiritual significance. Let us look at Assagioli's schema in more detail and see how it relates to the Tarot.

Natural symbols

The elements

The four elements, earth, air, fire and water appear in numerous combinations throughout the Tarot. They are represented through the four suits and represented again through the four fixed signs of the zodiac. The four suits represent the four functions of thinking, feeling, sensation and intuition. Additionally each of the elements carries its own extensive range of meaning and also appears in various forms. Water appears as stream, river, lake, pond, waterfall and icy waste. Fire appears as flame and sun. Air takes on a new meaning through wind and cloud. The earth and air together stand for heaven and earth as the backdrop against which the cards are set.

■ Look at the four suits: Discs, Swords, Rods, Cups.

■ Look at Trump I, the Magician. Here we find the elemental weapons as symbols of the four aspects of the psyche.

■ Look at Trump X, the Wheel of Fortune. Here we find four astrological signs as bull, lion, eagle and man.

■ Look at Trump XXI, the World. Here we find the four fixed signs of the zodiac as representatives of the indivisibility of creation.

What do the elements of earth, air, fire and water symbolise to you?

The sky

The sky is one of the first things a child draws. It is a universal symbol for the canopy beneath which we all live. The surreal yellow skies of, for example, the Rider-Waite Tarot pack represent the collective mind as a universal constant.

■ Look at Trump VII, the Chariot. Here the sky is represented by the canopy of the heavens.

What does the sky represent to you?

The Sun

The Sun is a universal symbol of life. It has appeared in the religious iconography of many peoples and represents both rebirth and resurrection. As the source of life, the Sun gives light and warmth to the world. Our seasons and daily pattern result from our relationship to the Sun. Sunrise and sunset carry different symbolic meanings. The east as the place of sunrise is still significant as the orientation for worship. The Sun is also represented through light and rays of light.

■ Look at Trump XIX, the Sun. Here we see the Sun radiating life, illumination and enlightenment.

■ Look at Trump XIII, Death. Here we see the rising Sun appearing between two pillars as a symbol of resurrection and renewal.

■ Look at Trump VII, the Chariot. Here we see the winged Sun disc as a symbol of spiritual liberation.

■ Look at Trump 0, the Fool. Here we see a white Sun as creative source of all life.

What does the Sun symbolise to you?

The Moon

The Moon has long fascinated skywatchers by its cyclic pattern of departure and return. Its qualities have been universally mythologised. The Moon has a real physical impact on our world through the tides. Moonlight is also related to the growth of plants and to the activity of creatures which swarm together. Early calendars used the Moon as a period of observable measurement. Of course, the moon has traditionally been connected with women through the menstrual cycle.

- Look at Trump II, the High Priestess. Here we see a lunar crescent set at the feet of the servant of the Goddess.
- Look at Trump VII, the Chariot. Here we see the charioteer who wears moon epaulettes to show that he has integrated both solar and lunar qualities.
- Look at Trump XVIII, the Moon. Here we see the path of biological evolution taking place under the light of the Moon.

What does the Moon symbolise to you?

The Stars

The stars have always fascinated. Today we reach out through observation and measurement. Earlier civilisations also watched the stars and created stories about them. The stars represent an enigmatic power which takes us beyond the confines of our world. Our own Sun of course is a star. There are many other such stars in the heavens. When we contemplate the night sky we find ourselves contemplating the infinite.

- Look at Trump VII, the Chariot. Here we see the canopy of stars which reminds us of the vastness of creation. The charioteer is also crowned with a star.
- Look at Trump III, the Empress. Here too the figure is crowned with stars.
- Look at Trump XVII, the Star. Here we see seven white stars surrounding a central larger star.

What do the stars represent to you?

Flowers – roses, lilies and sunflowers

The rose is another common symbol for love both human and divine. We find the symbolism of the rose in many traditions. The rose formed a central motif in Persian mysticism. The Virgin Mary is called the Rose of Heaven. The lily by contrast symbolises purity. It was by tradition the flower of the annunciation. The sunflower represents the Sun in shape and colour.

- Look at Trump 0, the Fool. Here the figure carries a white rose as he sets out on his journey.
- Look at Trump I, the Magician. Here we see both roses and lilies.
- Look at Trump XIII, Death. Here we find the five-petalled rose on the banner as a symbol of new life.
- Look at Trump V, the Hierophant. Here we once more see both roses and lilies upon the garments worn by the tonsured monks.
- Look at Trump XIX, the Sun. Here we see sunflowers.

What do flowers, roses, lilies and sunflowers represent to you?

The tree

The tree is an ancient symbol of growth, endurance and fertility. Its roots reach into the earth, its branches extend into the sky. Particular trees such as the oak have come to carry specialised symbolic overtones. The Tree of Life is an archetypal image of spiritual growth and nourishment. We find trees both real and stylised in the Tarot. The Suit of Wands shows us living branches to remind us that the energy portrayed is dynamic. The Suit of Pentacles is rich with trees and vegetation to remind us of the fertility of the earth.

- Look at Trump VI, the Lovers. Here we find two trees. Behind Eve we see the Tree of Life which is the Tree of the Knowledge of Good and Evil with its fruit and serpent. Behind Adam we see another tree with twelve lights ablaze. It is reminiscent of the Biblical burning bush, the tree that is alight with fire but does not burn.
- Look at Trump XII, the Hanged Man. Here we find another tree in the shape of a T. It represents the Tree of Sacrifice

whether Christian or pagan. Christ was crucified. Odin hung
on the World Tree Yggdrasil for nine nights.
- Look at Trump III, the Empress. Here we see lush vegetation
  and cypress trees which are sacred to Venus.

What do trees represent to you?

Animal symbols

The lion

Who can doubt the power and ferocity of the lion? It demands respect and
simultaneously evokes fear. The lion is an ambivalent symbol which
represents both the heights and depths to which raw power may be
directed.

- Look at Trump VIII, Strength. Here we see a woman holding
  open the mouth of a lion.

What does the lion symbolise to you?

The snake

The Biblical serpent is only too familiar to us as the instrument of
temptation but serpentine imagery is far older and more widespread than
Christianity. It represents mystery, wisdom and rebirth. Its coiling
represents creative potential and latency.

- Look at Trump I, the Magician. Here we see the serpent belt
  showing the tail grasped in the mouth to represent the
  injunction of silence.
- Look at Trump VI, the Lovers. Here we see the archetypal
  Adam and Eve with the serpent.

What does the serpent symbolise to you?

Mythological creatures

Fabulous creatures are the very essence of fable and fairy-tale. Griffins
and sphinxes, mermaids and monsters all represent flights of our
imagination. Each creature has its own qualities and characteristics.

- Look at Trump X, the Wheel of Fortune. Here we find two
  mythological creatures. One creature is a composite being

with a human body but the head of an animal, the other is clearly a sphinx.

■ Look at Trump VII, the Chariot. Here the chariot is drawn by two sphinxes.

What do mythological creatures represent to you?

Domestic animals

Unlike animals of legend and imagination, domesticated animals have a familiar reality. Dogs and cats have long been companions. The horse has shared a long history with humankind as a proud and intelligent animal. The donkey has always taken a humbler role as servant and carrier of goods.

■ Look at Trump 0, the Fool. Here the dog is found leaping beside the Fool.

■ Look at Trump XIX, the Sun. Here we see the donkey carrying the child.

■ Look at Trump XIII, Death. Here we see Death riding on a horse.

What do domestic animals symbolise to you?

Human symbols

The Tarot is full of human symbols. Look at the Court cards as representatives of humanity.

What do human symbols represent to you?

Man-made symbols

Man-made features and artefacts represent conscious decision-making and deliberate planning. Architecture itself has been used as a vehicle for sacred expression. Particular features can convey specific meaning. The bridge joins two different areas, the tunnel does the same but secretly. The stairway is the place of ascent or descent. A door permits entry, a window permits light to enter. Buildings such as a house or castle represent the self. Different rooms carry particular meaning too.

Look at Trump II, the High Priestess, Trump V, the Hierophant and Trump XI, Justice, where we find columns. This feature does not belong to domestic architecture. It is clearly reminiscent of the temple, the church or other buildings of state. The columns on either side of the High Priestess are deliberately depicted to suggest the two columns of the Temple of Solomon, Boaz and Jachin. There are too many man-made symbols to list but you can trace them for yourself.

What do these man-made symbols represent to you?

The path

The sequence of Tarot Trumps taken together represents a journey. It is not surprising that we should therefore find the recurring image of a path. The path itself is a universal symbol of the spiritual life. Buddhism speaks of the Lam Rim, the graduated path towards enlightenment. Yoga speaks of the Marga, the Path or Way. In the Western Mysteries the Path is to be found in the 22 Paths and the 10 Sephiroth of the Tree of Life.

- ■ Look at Trump 0, the Fool. Here we see that the figure is clearly about to take the first step. We do not see the path. The path lies ahead somewhere in the future.
- ■ Look at Trump VI, the Lovers. Here we see the path into life.
- ■ Look at Trump XIV, Temperance. Here we see the path stretching away into the far distance.
- ■ Look at Trump XVIII, the Moon. Here we see a pathway which emerges from a pool and finally disappears into a mountain range in the distance.

What does a path symbolise to you?

Religious and mythological symbols

The Tarot contains many traditional spiritual symbols which are found in religious iconography and mythological sources. Such references are very deep rooted. The mythology of the classical world is deeply ingrained within us through story and fable. The stories of classical gods and goddesses often relate to astrological themes, so this is an especially rich tradition which we may draw upon. Eastern religious symbols do not appear in the Rider-Waite pack which is based upon Western symbolism, but they have been used elsewhere.

- ■ Look at Trump III, the Empress. Here we see Mother Nature who is both Demeter and Venus.

■ Look at Trump XVII, the Star. Here we see Nuit the star goddess of the Egyptians.

■ Look at Trump V, the Hierophant. Here we see a priestly figure.

■ Look at the Ace of Cups. Here we see the archetypal Grail.

■ Look at Trump VI, the Lovers, Trump XX, Judgement and Trump XIV, Temperance where we find angelic figures as divine messengers.

■ Look at Trump XV, the Devil, where we see a widely recognised demonic image.

What do these traditional religious and mythological themes symbolise to you?

Teaching figures

What form does a spiritual teacher take in your mind? Do you see an ancient sage or a contemporary guru, a wise woman or a magician? The Tarot offers a wide range of teaching figures to us. Perhaps every character of the Major Arcana has something to teach us?

■ Look at Trump IX, the Hermit. Here is a representation of the Wise Old Man, the sage, the teacher, the guru. Here is Merlin or Gandalf.

■ Look at Trump II, the High Priestess. She is in service to the Goddess, the great feminine principle of wisdom.

What does a figure of wisdom represent to you?

Abstract symbols

The Tarot offers many abstract, geometric and number symbols.

Track them down for yourself and make notes on what these images represent to you.

Interacting with symbols

We have so far merely recognised and identified the fact that Psychosynthesis and the Tarot share the same symbolism to a remarkable degree. If we are to make real use of this information we need to turn it into practice. Teaching yourself Tarot and being taught by Tarot involves interaction. We have named the symbols that are worthy of special attention, now we need to make a personal approach. Each of the categories suggested by Assagioli can be approached through the intellect, the intuition and the creative imagination. You approach will depend upon the familiarity that you already possess. The important thing to remember is that this exploration is yours. Your personal answers and observations are what matters. You can approach the symbols that you find intellectually and intuitively. Working with even a single symbol can prove to be fascinating. It is like following a treasure trail into history, culture, mythology and art. Even the most obvious symbols have much to yield.

Guidelines for intellectual analysis:

- Choose a symbol. Record your thoughts, observations, comments and ideas. Repeat this process with other symbols.
- Compile your own categories of symbol, i.e. cosmic, regal authority, floral.
- Take each of the seven categories. Are you able to assign your own meaning to each of these symbols? If not, spend some time working with this list.
- Look at the symbols in conjunction with the cards on which they appear – make any notes.
- Take a single card and analyse its contents by symbol.
- If you have more than one Tarot pack take comparable cards and examine the different portrayals.
- Create your own dictionary of symbols.
- Take an abstract quality such as love, or compassion and express it as a symbol.

Guidelines for intuitive synthesis:

- Choose a single symbol as your theme. Begin to explore the meaning that it has for you. Do this by simple free association. Write down all the ideas, connections and associations which spring to mind for you.
- Close your eyes and create an internal image of the symbol you have chosen to work with. Allow yourself to repeat the same process of free association but try to summarise your

constellation of freely associated images into a single symbol.

- Take any chosen symbol and create it in your mind's eye. Hold the image clearly and watch the mind to see what impact holding this image has on you. Always note any particularly strong reactions.
- Use your own reactions and responses for further meditation.

From intuition towards gnosis

The images of the Tarot present an extraordinary opportunity for transpersonal growth. Psychosynthesis offers techniques. Tarot offers highly relevant symbols. There is an extraordinary accord of approach. When approaching the Tarot through creative visualisation and internal dialogue we are bordering upon what Psychosynthesis refers to as the transcendent, the realm of the superconscious. Assagioli reminds us that 'the higher realm has been known throughout the ages'. [5] This is the realm of the collective rather than the personal, it is the place of the great and enduring themes of human life such as wisdom, truth and love. Assagioli's practical advice holds the authority of experience. It is suggested that when we seek spiritual counsel

> ... we must seek the teacher within. It is necessary to make an inner journey, more exactly an ascent to the various levels of the conscious and superconscious psyche to approach this inner teacher and then in the imagination to simply state the problem, talking to the imagined teacher realistically as if he were a living person and as in everyday conversation courteously awaiting a response.[6]

It is only possible to take these suggestions seriously and give them credence when we fully understand that we are not interacting with pictures on card but through these images with the archetypal forces which are within ourselves. Such approaches are remarkably similar to the techniques employed by the Golden Dawn and its successors. Transpersonal humanistic psychology has much in common with the psychological and spiritual techniques of the Mystery Schools of past and present. Assagioli's description of the approach to the inner teacher

presents us with an important key. Finding the teacher within is a
significant and moving personal experience. The following guidelines
explain the technique. Reaching inner dialogue is as much about
surrendering as striving. It is achieved most easily by adult suspension of
disbelief and by finding a childlike willingness to enter the world of the
imagination. Never hurry this inner work. Leave time for assimilation and
integration between your approaches. In accordance with a Mysterys
teaching, 'Make haste slowly'.

1 **Seek the teacher within**: Select the card you wish to work with.
  Have it in front of you.
2 **Make an inner journey**: Enter a meditative state and visualise the
  card clearly in your mind.
3 **Ascend to the various levels of the conscious and superconscious
  psyche**: Allow the image to grow so that the frame of the card
  becomes a doorway.
4 **Approach this inner teacher**: Step into the image. Bring the Tarot
  landscape to life as vividly as possible. See the character as
  realistically as possible.
5 **In the imagination simply state the problem**: Deepen your
  meditative state. Speak from the heart. Ask what you need to learn
  from this character.
6 **Talk to the imagined teacher realistically as if he/she were a
  living person**: Always be respectful when journeying in the inner
  world. Inner experience can produce responses in everyday life.
7 **Courteously await a response**: Keep your mind open to any
  response such as words, sounds, actions or gestures.
8 When the meditation is finished, step back through the image.
  Reduce it to a proper size. Return all images to a passive state and
  finally dissolve all images.
9 Record your experiences straight away.

Summary

■ You have connected the symbols of the Tarot with the
  symbols presented through Psychosynthesis.
■ You have begun to work with the symbols of the Tarot at
  your own pace both intellectually and intuitively.

4 THE ELEMENTAL FOUNDATION

The four elements are particularly useful in understanding the essential nature of any individual's psychological make-up.

Stephen Arroyo, *Astrology*, *Psychology and the Four Elements*

The elements and the Tarot

As a child learns to read words slowly and through practice, so reading pictures also calls for familiarity. As a child learns to recognise both individual letters and the shape of words, we also need to recognise and decode the many symbols which make up the language of Tarot. We will begin with the building blocks of Tarot, namely the four elements – earth, air, fire and water. These are our foundation. It should be no surprise to find that the elements of nature have appeared repeatedly throughout the spiritual traditions of the world. Look at the world around you. The ground is below, fire is far above, air surrounds you, water falls upon you. These universals have etched themselves deeply into human consciousness in all their numerous forms and manifestations.

Let us see where contemplation of earth, air, fire and water can lead us. We separate the elements for our own cerebral purpose. In reality there is only interdependence. The earth is sustained by water, warmth and clean air. Water is absorbed into the earth and evaporated invisibly into the air to later appear as droplets again. The air contains tiny particles of once solid substances. Cosmic fire creates the building blocks of the future through constant atomic explosion.

The system of elemental symbolism which we find embedded in the structure of the Tarot is not, however, intended as a literal description of the world in which we live. It is intended to function as a symbolic vehicle of expression. Symbolic thinking awakens the mind. Specific symbols lead the mind towards realisation. These four elements are, of course, only described as elements in the language of metaphysics. Science looks to the periodic table for its elements. Ultimately all such definitions prove to be limited constructs for our tangibly solid world proves to be a projection from a bizarre sub-atomic substratum. Mystical traditions have long recognised this dual reality as appearance and illusion, matter and energy. The deeper reality has many names. It is often called 'Akasa' and thought of as the fifth element. It represents the mystery at the heart of life itself. The Tarot shows us the four elements as disc, sword, wand and cup. It also shows us the four elements as the four fixed signs of the zodiac: Taurus, Aquarius, Leo and Scorpio in the form of bull, man, lion and eagle respectively. It does not show us the fifth element, Akasa, directly. We have to find it for ourselves in the true spirit of the quest. Akasa is ever present. It is invisible until the moment of personal realisation. The Tarot has the power to awaken us to Akasa. Although the Tarot explicitly utilises the four elements in a system of correspondences, it implicitly recognises the fifth element too. If the Minor Arcana correlates to the four elements, then the Major Arcana represents Akasa, the indefinable spirit of life itself.

As an exercise, sort the Tarot pack into its five sets, the four suits and the Major Arcana. Lay these five side by side and spread the sets out in their vertical rows (see Figure 4.1).

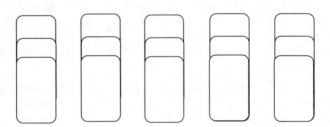

Figure 4.1   Earth, Air, Fire, Water and Akasa

Contemplate this symbolic arrangement. However, there is something curiously unsatisfying about linear models which always enforce both beginnings and endings. Laying out the Tarot in this fashion shows us only a paucity of thought and imagination. In effect we have created little more than a pictorial list. So, now rearrange the same four suits as four arms radiating from a central point and place the 22 cards of the Major

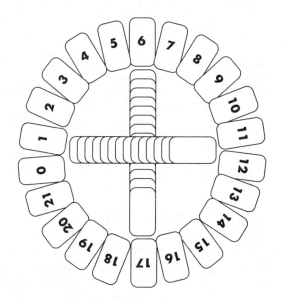

Figure 4.2   The circle of life

Arcana around the periphery (see Figure 4.2). Contemplate this symbolic arrangement. We have now created a much richer pattern which produces both the circle and the cross in combination. Let us offer this new image to the intuition:

- Contemplate the space at the central point. What does this represent to you?
- Contemplate the equal-armed cross. What does this image signify to you?
- Contemplate the circle. What does this mean to you?
- Contemplate the circle and the cross as a unified symbol. What does this mean to you?
- Compare this pattern with the linear pattern. Which arrangement do you find more satisfying?

The power of symbolic thought lies in its flexibility. A single idea can be expressed in various symbolic forms. The more fluent you become in the language of symbol, the more effectively you will understand the

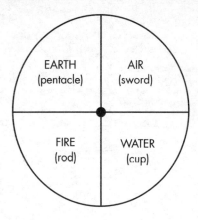

Figure 4.3   Unity and diversity

language of Tarot. Let us express what we have already discovered in other ways. First, draw a circle and divide it into four quarters. Place the name of each element and its related symbol in each quarter. Mark the central point in your own way with either a word or an image (see Figure 4.3). Contemplate this image. Next, draw a five-pointed star, which is also known as a pentagram. Each of the points of the star represents one of the elements, earth, air, fire, water and spirit (see Figure 4.4). Contemplate this image. Finally, draw a five-pointed star set within a circle (see Figure 4.5). Contemplate this image.

Figure 4.4   The star of the elements

Figure 4.5   The pentacle

The elements within

The symbol of the five-pointed star which has been used to describe the
five elements also serves to remind us that the elements are by
correspondence also found within us. Earth, air, fire and water are easily
located in the outer world. What parts of your own being could be likened
to the characteristic qualities of earth, air, fire, water and spirit?

- What part of your being could be described as earthy?
- What part of your being could be described as airy?
- What part of your being could be described as fiery?
- What part of your being could be described as watery?
- What part of your being could be described as spiritual?

See if you agree with the following schema:

- The Element of Earth represents our interactions with the
  world as a physical system, the Function of Sensation and
  the Body.
- The Element of Air represents our communication with
  others, the Function of the Intellect and the concrete Mind.
- The Element of Fire represents our inspired drive in life, the
  Function of the Intuition.

■ The Element of Water represents our ability to relate through the emotions, the Function of Feeling and the Heart.

■ The Element of Akasa represents the totality of being which functions through the four psychological functions.

Even this simple schema has much to yield through meditation. Earth as the densest of the elements well represents the body which is the most dense expression of our own being. The mind which is invisible is well represented by air which is omnipresent yet without form. The element of water is easily associated with our feelings, which belong to the heart. The element of fire represents the will to be and the self-expressive drive in life.

The Four Holy Kerubs

In the Major Arcana, we find the elemental images of Earth, Air, Fire and Water in Trump XXI, the World, and Trump X, the Wheel of Fortune. In both Trumps we see Taurus, Aquarius, Leo and Scorpio. These are the four fixed signs of the zodiac. Additionally, these same images are referred to as the Four Holy Kerubs. These suggest the creative powers of the universe at work on the inner side of creation. We will approach this idea through meditation. Look at both Tarot Trump X and Tarot Trump XXI. Both share the same astrological symbolism. In each of the corners you will see one of the Four Holy Kerubs. Choose one of these Trumps to be your guide. The order in which you encounter the elemental powers is not significant. Once again do not rush these encounters. Allow plenty of time between encounters for assimilation and integration.

The Kerub of Earth – Taurus

I seek myself through what I have.

Taurus is the second sign of the zodiac. It is symbolised by the bull. Unlike the lion which represents the wild and the untamed, the bull stands for agriculture and the organisation of nature. It seems curious that we should use the word, 'husbandry' to describe this relationship with nature as it implies the closeness of a marriage. With husbandry comes meat and milk, leather and process, breeding and birthing, planting and harvesting. As nature's bounty becomes our own, a new relationship with the world around us emerges. We can see something of this relationship through the following meditation.

Enter your own state of meditation and call the full image to mind within the frame of the card. Allow the frame to expand and become as an open doorway. Through the open doorway, you can only glimpse the head of the bull but as you watch, the bull walks into full view. You take a step towards the doorway and then pass through.

Find yourself approaching the Taurean bull. His bulk and size are formidable. You do not even reach his shoulder. You cannot fail to be aware of his strength and physical presence. You approach quietly and with care, the huge head turns towards you, your eyes meet and you feel great depth and compassion. This gentleness is reassuring and you move closer. The bull turns towards you and nuzzles into your face. You begin to feel relaxed and safe. The bull drops onto his forelocks and you know it is time to climb on his back. You settle yourself into the natural saddle of his back and he sets off. At once you are in an open landscape of green hills and rolling fields. Ahead of you is a winding path set between an avenue of tall poplars. Your guide strolls along at a gentle pace. There is time to enjoy the scenery. Sunlight filters through the trees. There is much to see if you are really observant; tiny insects rise at the approach of the bull. Bright flowers grow in the banks along the path. On either side of the path, fields of wheat are growing. Still green, the ears of wheat are not fully ripe but you know that with warmth and water the harvest will come. You remember the classical mother of the corn Ceres or Demeter and you reflect upon the significance of wheat in the shared history of peoples. The gifts of agriculture were once honoured with ceremony and due respect. The harvest was once far more than merely gathering in the crop. It was time for the shared honouring of the gifts of the land. Briefly, images of peoples now long gone come into your mind. You see the hard toil of cutting and binding, the shared labour of carrying and taking, the sense of communal spirit working with common cause. You momentarily hear their voices raised in song. Through the evocation of memory, you see the last sheaf standing in the middle of the field. It is the prepared place for the spirit of the corn, a sign of respect to the land itself. You continue to muse on things past, your guide moves on.

The air seems to be warming. You sense a change in the land itself and the people who have lived in relationship with the earth here. Now you are in vineyard country. See the rows of vines running up hill and across valley. Here is the long labour of a people devoted to the care of the land and its bounty. Your mind turns to wine and its place in the shared history of peoples and places. The ancient divinities of the wine harvest, Dionysus and Bacchus fleetingly pass into your mind. Your reverie is interrupted by the joyful sound of festivities a little way off. A procession is coming down the hill. You see them now. Banners are held aloft. Young girls dressed in white balance trays of grapes on their heads, old men with weather-worn faces follow. Women in black carry huge baskets, children excitedly move in and out of their elders. Here is a community moving as one. The procession reaches you and halts in greeting. Immediately a bottle is drawn up from a basket and opened. A glazed cup is found and you know you are being offered the best of last year's harvest. You raise your cup in salute to these people and their labour. As you drink the villagers break into spontaneous applause at your gesture. You return your cup with thanks. Another cup is poured full to the brim and then with reverent gesture poured onto the ground. The wine is returned to the earth with thanks. The villagers now set off and your guide moves on.

Now the path climbs upwards again. The landscape seems to be changing. The air grows hotter. The land feels dry, baked from the continuous power of the sun. The wine makes you feel drowsy in the heat and you allow yourself to drift into reverie as you are rocked in rhythmic motion by the steady gait of your guide beneath you. You are jolted into awakening, your guide has come to a standstill. Now you pay attention to new surroundings. You have arrived in a high place overlooking a timeless settlement of whitened houses. The sun beats down as it has always done here. Looking around you see yourself surrounded by gnarled ancient trees set in stony ground. You have come to an olive grove, unchanged through time. Something catches your eye in the sunlight. A small statue stands on an outcrop of rock close to a tree. Here is Athena, the traditional bestower of the olive tree and patroness of the once great city of Athens. It seems appropriate that her name should be remembered here in the olive grove. You reach out to an overhanging bough and pluck a sprig of olive to carry away in memory. Will you remember to plant something real to remind you of this inner journey?

From inside your mind, you hear the words. 'Have you seen earth?' You reply and you know that your journey is over. Scenery fades, inner landscapes dissolve away. Find yourself returned to your starting point. You dismount and mentally take a step back through the frame. Allow all images to settle and then be dissolved in your mind. Make any notes on your inner experiences.

The Kerub of Air – Aquarius

I seek myself through humanity.

Aquarius is the eleventh sign of the zodiac. It is symbolised by the water carrier though it is an air sign. This often leads to some confusion but these are the waters of cosmic mind. The water bearer kneels in a gesture of service. The great urn rests on one shoulder and the contents overflow like a great flood. This symbolism is rather different from that of bull, lion or eagle which are images taken from nature. Aquarius is represented by humanity itself. The water bearer is the human in service to humanity. The urn, like magical containers in fairy-tales, is never empty but ever full yet constantly emptying itself. It pours out inspiration and creativity, possibility and vision to those whose hearts and minds have space to hold such rich waters. We too may feel a brief moment of inspiration through the following meditation.

Enter your own state of meditation. Call the image of your chosen Trump to mind. Step through the doorway of the card. See the human head and watch the rest of the body form. Choose whether you would like your guide to take male or female guise. Gender should not be an issue as the guide stands for humanity but you can choose. Your guide reaches out and takes you by the hand. A mist begins to swirl and gather around your feet. It rises like smoke until you are both engulfed by it. It is so dense that you can no longer see a face but you still feel a hand holding yours. You wonder about this mist which has arisen from nowhere. If this element represents the human mind, what is this vapour other than a level of mind without clarity? Here is confusion, indecision, vacillation and uncertainty. The desire for clarity arises in your mind. Here in the fog the way forward is unclear. Your own thought seems to make a difference for a space appears around your body. You maintain your thought with purpose and the space continues to spread; now your guide seems to be assisting with a powerful thought, for you see the mist visibly retreating. It seems to shrink away.

Your guide begins to enter a state of deep concentration which is meditation. This deep state brings a great sense of peace and calm to you too. The whole atmosphere of your shared space has become infused by these radiating thoughts. You suddenly feel that you are sharing thoughts with your guide. Within your own mind, you hear a voice arising. 'I will show you Air.' You feel that your guide knows what is in your mind. You wonder whether your own thoughts are clear or muddied and confused. You sense a deep shift taking place between you. It is as if the air itself has been transformed into shared mind. You feel yourself carried upon the current of this greater mind which feels substantial and utterly real. As you watch your guide in a state of deep absorption, you sense a serenity and peacefulness which lies beyond the busy chatter of intellectual activity. Though your guide is deeply absorbed in mind, you feel certain that you both share the same awareness. Without any visible sign of acknowledgement, you nevertheless sense a deep recognition between you. The shared space between you now seems very bright and clear, it almost feels alive. You become very aware of the atmosphere enclosing you both. Your mind now feels very open and expanded, it is not filled by idle and meaningless thoughts but lies still and receptive. This expanded state of being is quite different from the normal state of awareness. You sense a certainty and immediacy which defy the normal processes of thinking. In your state of openness, you become aware that the space around you is being subtly infused by colour. You sense rose pinks, deep blues, violet, gold, magenta and turquoise. You realise that these are the manifestations of pure mind as colour. Here is the mind of your guide held steadfast, pure and rendered utterly real. You allow yourself to bathe in these colours for each brings a quality of being, you bathe in serenity, calm and peace. One colour seems especially significant so you allow yourself to rest within it for as long as you need. This colour will surely bring you a clear inspiration. You hear the words, 'Have you seen Air?' You make your reply.

Now you feel your guide withdrawing from this state. The colours fade. The atmosphere relaxes. Allow yourself to step back through the frame. Allow everything to settle. Allow all the images to be dissolved. Make notes on your experience.

The Kerub of Fire – Leo

> I seek myself through what I create.

Leo is the fifth sign of the zodiac. It is symbolised by the heart. If we combine the symbolism of the lion with that of the heart we arrive at the idea of the lionheart which is bold, fearless, confident, honest and genuine. It is a heart given in service to the greater good. It is a kingship given in service. We hope to catch something of these leonine qualities through the following meditation.

Ensure that you can re-create the image of your chosen Trump in your mind's eye. Enter your own state of meditation and call the full image to mind within the frame of the card. Allow the frame to expand and become as an open doorway. Through the open doorway, you can only glimpse the head of the lion, but as you watch the lion walks into full view and you are possibly reminded in some way of Aslan. You take a step towards the doorway and then pass through. The lion stands before you and you remember that here is one of the four Holy Kerubs rather than the beast of nature. The lion turns towards you, your eyes meet in a deep gaze which embodies both wisdom and love. You are now perfectly at ease here.

The lion takes a step towards you. His huge head and mane rub against you. You are getting to know one another. He drops his front legs and it seems only natural that now you should climb upon his back. The lion sets off at a walking pace. You and he seem to be attuned to one another's thoughts. 'I will show you Fire.' You hear these words directly into your mind. As you walk on, the air seems to be warming rapidly. Looking up you see a brilliant Sun in the sky. Rays of light shine like a halo. The Sun is a fire beyond comprehension. It is your cosmic heart. The lion now begins to break into a run. You realise that he runs because the ground beneath is hot to the touch. Vapour and gas gush from the ground. A strange smell fills the air, it is sulphur carried on the air. The landscape around you now is unworldly and strange; pools of liquid earth bubble and boil, the ground spits and hisses. The sky is now dark and foreboding. A flash of lightning breaks the sky with the crack of electrical fire. Against the skyline you see the outline of volcanoes. Fire is everywhere. In this primeval landscape are the seeds of the future. Fire is the birthplace of the distant future. It is the alchemical cauldron which is the birthplace of becoming. The great lion beneath you has increased his pace once again, his feet hardly seem to touch the ground at all. You now seem to rise above the ground out of harm's way. Sparks fly and plumes of smoke rise, the ground is molten, it flows as a river of fire beneath you. As you watch, a pillar of fire is building against the background of the sky. It is a rod of flame which bridges heaven and earth. Sparks fly everywhere. Each tiny spark like a seed has the power to ignite a great flame. A spark from this moment of creation enters your heart. It brings a deep warmth, you understand what it means to be warm hearted. Will you nurture the tiny flame within you, or will it die and grow cold? You hear the words, 'Have you seen Fire?' You give your reply.

Your guide turns and in changing direction you know that you are now moving away from elemental fire and slowly returning to your starting place. You feel a cooling breeze against your body. Time passes swiftly until there is a gentle jolt and your guide sets you down where you began. You allow yourself to rest and ponder your inner experiences. You dismount and withdraw from the scene by mentally stepping back through the door frame. Allow the images to settle back into two dimensions once more. Finally dissolve all the images that you have created. Record your experiences as soon as possible.

The Kerub of Water – Scorpio

I seek myself through what I desire.

Scorpio is the eighth sign of the zodiac. Unusually it is symbolised by two signs, the scorpion and the eagle. The scorpion brings death. It can steal a life in a moment. Its unnerving power reminds us of the fragility of life. Imagine being in a darkened room with a loose scorpion. Who would not face up to the fundamental questions of life and death in that moment? Scorpio is the awakener. Once awakened, however, consciousness may soar through the symbolism of the high flying eagle which is the watcher on high. We may glimpse something of this transformation through the following meditation.

Have the image of the chosen Trump clearly in your mind. Expand the frame and allow it to become a doorway. See yourself stepping through. Allow your attention to focus on the being of the eagle. First you see only the head clearly but as you watch the rest comes into view. The eagle's head turns towards you and you feel a keen eye upon you. This eye is sharp. Yet in this sharpness there is clarity and depth of vision. You feel relieved that you are not asked to ride upon the scorpion which also symbolises the power of Scorpio in its lower aspect. Instead you will ride the high flying eagle, symbol of the highest functions of Scorpionic power.

The eagle seems to have read your mind; wings are spread ready for you. You approach and climb up, nestling yourself into the feathered back. At once the eagle rises high. You hear the words, 'I will show you Water.' You soar into the clouds. You are surrounded by cloud. As you pass through this unfamiliar realm you realise that it is here that rain is born. Now you feel yourself descending. The clouds part and there beneath you lies the great ocean. As far as the eye can see in every direction there is water and you realise that most of the earth is covered by water. Out of the corner of your eye, you see movement close to the surface. Your guide instinctively takes you closer. Whales are breaching. You see their majestic forms rising and falling. Your heart responds to these creatures. You are awakened to a depth of feeling within yourself. You want to communicate your feelings to them, to let them know how you feel at this moment. You simply let waves of love flow from your heart and mind. As the waves upon the sea merge one into another, so the love which you send out flows in waves which merge and blend one into another. Your guide moves on, the school of whales is already behind you. You ride effortlessly over the ocean far below. You realise that beneath the surface lies a hidden kingdom teeming with a life of its own.

You lose all sense of time, you fly on and on. How much better to ride the high flying eagle and gain the expansive overview than to be astride the earth-bound scorpion with limited perspective. In the distance you see land rising from the sea. Soon you are within sight of the coastline. Your guide slows down and you pass along the tide line. You reflect on the daily tidal rhythm which lifts the waters from the land like an unseen hand. In this great ebb and flow of the waters of life, you see mirrored the lesser rising and fallings of life's cycles. Like the tide itself, we ride on invisible currents which carry us towards unknown destinations and new shores. Water exists within our bodies, we have a natural resonance to its rhythms.

Now you pass inland where water brings fertility and life to its people. You see irrigation channels cut with great care. You see pools and streams like blue veins in the body of the land. You see the ancient water wheels still standing in the landscape. You pass on, now picking up speed. Ahead of you in the far distance is a great swathe of blue water. Here is one of the great rivers of the world. Here is the Nile, the life blood of an ancient civilisation. You turn so that you ride above the Nile following its length as it cuts into the land. On either side a swathe of green forms a lush covering. But suddenly the living green finishes and gives way to the barren grip of the desert. You remember that it was the annual rising of the Nile which gave the gift of life. The annual flood was known as the tears of Isis, the tears of the goddess so beloved by the Egyptians. These divine tears nourished the national spirit. The human tear gives life too for in our tears all is dissolved. When feelings flow the heart is opened. Only the stony hearted cannot weep. Now you allow yourself to remember the last time you cried. As you do so a single tear condenses in the heart space and reminds you that you can still cry for yourself and others. Your guide turns and you know your journey is drawing to its close. 'Have you seen Water?' You make your reply.

Your guide sets you down where you began. You dismount and withdraw from the scene by mentally stepping back through the door frame. When you have withdrawn allow the images to settle back into two dimensions once more. Dissolve all the images that you have created. Record your experiences as soon as possible.

These meditations will bring you closer to an intuitive understanding of the elemental powers expressed through the Tarot. Although the four suits and the four fixed signs of the zodiac are the most obvious elemental expressions, the Tarot includes more subtle reference to elemental energies through both Qabalah and astrology. We have already encountered Taurus, Leo, Scorpio and Aquarius. The remaining signs and planets, each with an elemental signature, also have a place in the Tarot.

Astrology and the elements

Tarot and astrology, as maps of consciousness are two of the many keys in the human journey of evolvement. Both are tools for drawing us inward to the collective unconscious. Both are symbolic metaphysical languages that communicate all of life's energies.

Karen La Puma, *Charting the New Age by Astrological Tarot*

Contemporary Tarot has now incorporated much astrological symbolism mainly through its relationship with Qabalah which rejoices in the law of correspondences. As the astrological correspondences serve to deepen our understanding of the cards there is value in relating the two systems. The 22 cards of the Major Arcana are allocated to the 12 signs of the zodiac and the ten planets. The individual cards of the Minor Arcana also have astrological identities which combine planets and signs. Each of the 78 Tarot cards therefore carries an astrological character which is derived from zodiacal and planetary qualities.

Let us now look at the way in which the elemental characteristics of the astrological signs relate to the 22 Trumps of the Major Arcana. The twelve signs of the zodiac are divided into four groups:

- **Earth signs**: Capricorn, Taurus, Virgo.
- **Air signs**: Libra, Aquarius, Gemini.
- **Fire signs**: Aries, Leo, Sagittarius.
- **Water signs**: Cancer, Scorpio, Pisces.

Each of the four triplicities is attributed qualities and characteristics which exemplify the nature of the elemental energy:

- **The Earth triplicity**: The Earth signs are related to organisation in the physical world. Earth signs provide necessities, bestow opportunities, organise resources, have a deep-rooted natural understanding, show a practical intelligence, recognise potential, use resources creatively.
- **The Air triplicity**: The Air signs are related to mind, the realm of ideas and our ability to communicate what we think. Air signs are co-operative, gregarious, humane, inspirational, quick, intelligent, imaginative, objective and inventive.
- **The Fire triplicity**: The Fire signs are related to will and drive in the world. Fire signs are courageous, self-assertive, idealistic, visionary, helpful, creative, active, ardent and strong-minded.
- **The Water triplicity**: The Water signs are related to feelings and emotions. Water signs are compassionate, understanding, sensitive, impressionable, artistic, romantic and caring.

Additionally, the 12 signs are each described as being either cardinal, fixed or mutable. Cardinal signs initiate. Fixed signs stabilise. Mutable signs offer adaptability.

- **Cardinal signs**: Aries, Cancer, Capricorn, Libra.
- **Fixed signs**: Taurus, Aquarius, Leo, Scorpio.
- **Mutable signs**: Gemini, Pisces, Virgo, Sagittarius.

The signs of the zodiac are allocated to the Major Arcana in the following way:

- **Aries (Fire)**: the Emperor.
- **Taurus (Earth)**: the Hierophant.
- **Gemini (Air)**: the Lovers.
- **Cancer (Water)**: the Chariot.
- **Leo (Fire)**: Strength.
- **Virgo (Earth)**: the Hermit.
- **Libra (Air)**: Justice.
- **Scorpio (Water)**: Death.
- **Sagittarius (Fire)**: Temperance.
- **Capricorn (Earth)**: the Devil.
- **Aquarius (Air)**: the Star.
- **Pisces (Water)**: the Moon.

In order to understand how the zodiacal qualities enrich the cards to which they have been assigned we need to understand the basic characteristics assigned to each sign. We can once more apply our learning schema. If astrology is a new field for you, feed the intellectual mind by reading about the nature and characteristics of the sign. Then move on to consider the individual card itself. When your understanding of the astrological significance has become internalised, you will find it easy and natural to draw upon this knowledge through insight and wise application.

- **Aries – Cardinal Fire – symbolised by the ram**: Courageous, bold, direct, decisive, takes initiative, has natural qualities of leadership.

  In what way do the qualities assigned to Aries enrich and support the meaning of Trump IV, the Emperor?

■ **Taurus – Fixed Earth – symbolised by the bull**: Steadfast, sensitive, understanding, productive, generous, composed, patient, calm.

In what way do the qualities assigned to Taurus enrich and support the meaning of Trump V, the Hierophant?

■ **Gemini – Mutable Air – symbolised by the twins**: Light-hearted, cheerful, intelligent, versatile, adaptable.

In what way do the qualities assigned to Gemini enrich and support the meaning of Trump VI, the Lovers?

■ **Cancer – Cardinal Water – symbolised by the crab**: Home loving, cares for others, empathic, sensitive, psychic, impressionable.

In what way do the qualities assigned to Cancer enrich and support the meaning of Trump VII, the Chariot?

■ **Leo – Fixed Fire – symbolised by the lion**: Self-assured, bold, progressive, warm, sincere, protective, artistic, loves universally.

In what way do the qualities assigned to Leo enrich and support the meaning of Trump VIII, Strength?

■ **Virgo – Mutable Earth – symbolised by the maiden**: Helpful, unassuming, self-reliant, dependable, unselfish, serves others.

In what way do the qualities assigned to Virgo enrich and support the meaning of Trump IX, the Hermit?

■ **Libra – Cardinal Air – symbolised by the scales**: Impartial, balanced, fair minded, good at partnerships, sees both sides of any dispute.

In what way do the qualities assigned to Libra enrich and support the meaning of Trump XI, Justice?

■ **Scorpio – Fixed Water – symbolised by the scorpion and the eagle**: Deep, mystical, questing, far seeing, searching, a need to probe the fundamental issues of life.

In what way do the qualities assigned to Scorpio enrich and support the meaning of Trump XIII, Death?

■ **Sagittarius – Mutable Fire – symbolised by the archer**:
Forward looking, an enquiring mind, natural curiosity, quick to learn, good teachers.

In what way do the qualities assigned to Sagittarius enrich and support the meaning of Trump XIV, Temperance?

■ **Capricorn – Cardinal Earth – symbolised by the goat**:
Organised, practical, resourceful, traditional, hardworking, loyal, good leaders.

In what way do the qualities assigned to Capricorn enrich and support the meaning of Trump XV, the Devil?

■ **Aquarius – Fixed Air – symbolised by the water bearer**:
Intuitive, strives for brotherhood, loyal to a cause, loves humanity, gregarious, social.

In what way do the qualities assigned to Aquarius enrich and support the meaning of Trump XVII, the Star?

■ **Pisces – Mutable Water – symbolised by the two fishes**:
Unselfish, visionary, imaginative, spiritual, creative, sensitive.

In what way do the qualities assigned to Pisces enrich and support the meaning of Trump XVIII, the Moon?

The Qabalah, the Tarot and the elements

It is impossible to ignore the Qabalistic principles that have become woven into the fabric of Tarot. Despite the fact that Qabalah is a complex metaphysical philosophy, we may examine a single significant idea, namely the Tetragrammaton. This has been interwoven with Tarot since the days of Elphas Levi and the nineteenth-century French esoteric movement which created a link between the four letters of the Holy Name of God, Y-H-V-H and the four elements. To understand this relationship better, we might like to think of a child's delight in creating codes. Letters become translated into numbers, other letters or even shapes. The Hebrew alphabet is a ready-made code. Unlike our own language where letters carry only a phonetic value, Hebrew is a sacred language. The difference is enormous. Every Hebrew letter is itself a symbol and carries further symbolism through a corresponding number. A single word can convey a depth of meaning which is not apparent to the uninitiated who see only the written signs. Let us now look at the four letters of the holy name, Y-H-V-H. This is spelled with the letters Yod, He, Vau and a repeated He, which is referred to as the He final. The Tetragrammaton is treated with much reverence and respect. By aligning aspects of the Tarot with this most sacred sign, we align ourselves to the most sacred, hidden and subtle processes within creation. Each of the four letters carries an elemental value.

> To the Yod, Fire is ascribed
> To the He, Water is ascribed
> To the Vau, Air is ascribed
> To the He (final), Earth is ascribed

This correspondence means that whenever these letters appear as part of a word, the elemental power is considered to be present. As every letter of the alphabet carries its own symbolism, words immediately become translated into ideas. The Divine Name, which is considered too holy to be spoken aloud, embraces earth, air, fire and water. In other words the divine name includes the whole of creation. The four elements and the four letters of the sacred name seemed inevitably destined to be wedded one to the other. Although this relationship may seem obscure, even artificial, it has done much to deepen the symbolism of the Tarot. We can apply this formula too, using the understanding that you have already gained:

- Which suit might be attributed to Yod?
- Which suit might be attributed to He?
- Which suit might be attributed to Vau?
- Which suit might be attributed to He final?

Summary

- You have experienced each of the four elemental qualities through meditation.
- You have seen how astrology reinforces and expands the elemental correspondence.
- You have seen how the Tetragrammaton and the Tarot can be philosophically related.

5 | THE TAROT COURT

The court cards of the Tarot traditionally represent various human personality types, in keeping with their zodiacal assignations but above and beyond this, they are elemental archetypes. They are linked to a broad spectrum of natural forces.

Gary Ross, *The Court Cards – Nature's Archetypes*

The royal courts

The royal court has a diminished meaning today in the age of democratic rule but if we relate Tarot to fifteenth-century Italy where it originated we can appreciate the relevance of the courtly characters. The symbols of royal authority carried great weight. Thrones, sceptres, wands, heraldic devices and crowns once conveyed a power in the real world. The royal court revolved around the person of the king who was the centre of influence and often wielded the power of life and death. The queen was also a person of great significance, possibly a power behind the throne but on occasion a ruler in her own right. The figure of the knight may belong more to the ideals of chivalry than the reality of territorial squabbles but we see echoes of both worldly power and spiritual intent in this character. The page is clearly the junior here, a figure in service and training to the greater powers.

It has to be said that although this quaternary is maintained in the majority of the Tarot Courts, the Golden Dawn introduced a new symbology which substituted the figure of the king with that of the knight. The dynamic energy elsewhere attributed to the role of the king was transferred to the figure of knight. Crowley followed this substitution in his own *Book of Thoth* and depicted this energy with stunning visual presence. His knights are each represented on horseback and clad in armour: 'Their action is swift and violent but transient.' In keeping with the Qabalistic formula of the Tetragrammaton, the knight corresponded to the letter *Yod*, which represents the first outpouring of fiery dynamic energy. In *The Book of Thoth*, the role of the queen remains much the same as elsewhere: 'They are the complement of the knights, they receive, ferment and transmit the original energy of their knight, they are represented as seated on thrones.' The queens are attributed to the second letter of the Tetragrammaton, He which signifies elemental water. Having replaced the king by the figure of the knight Crowley now makes use of other traditional royal personages, the prince and princess. The princes are attributed to the third letter of the Tetragrammaton, *Vau*, elemental air. The prince is represented upon a chariot as the second dynamic energy. Finally we find the princesses who represent: 'The ultimate issue of the original energy in its completion and crystallisation, its materialisation.'[1] They are attributed to the fourth quadrant of the Tetragrammaton, the He final, representing elemental earth. Crowley's metaphysics may or may not appeal to you. The Thoth pack remains an outstanding Tarot. If you are attracted to it, look at the Tarot court differently at the outset.

Let us become attuned to the archetypal energy of the Tarot courts.

The King at Court

I am the power holder who bestows royal largesse through gift or favour. The king rules the kingdom. I have the power to establish laws and pass judgements. When my power is expressed through the figure of the knight you see my ability to change lives and circumstances with swift action. Whether called king or knight, I am the centre of court life. I am the primal energy. I am expected to rule well and wisely. A foolish king is never loved. As history shows kings have not always succeeded in ruling wisely and well. The temptations of power are great, so each of the four kings exemplifies the failings and negative qualities of the powers represented by the suit. Heavy is the head that wears the crown.

The Queen at Court

I am the queen at court. I am often seen as the power behind the throne. But my role is considerable. I consolidate and build, establish and maintain. I take the germ of an idea and turn it into something real. I know how to implement a possibility and turn it into a lasting contribution. My patronage brings long-term benefits and growth. I bring a consolidating presence. I am your friend at court.

The Knight at Court

I am the champion of the court where the values of chivalry count for something. I uphold the honour of the court and may wear the colours of the queen. I am seen as a heroic figure. I am the knight who sets out at the behest of my patron. I go into the world to find fulfilment. I offer the total commitment to the powers of the suit. All my energies are directed upon the task in hand. When I appear in the guise of the prince, I set out to take the values of the court into new realms and dimensions. I carry the authority and weight of the court with me.

The Page at Court

I am the youngest member of the Tarot court. As page I am in service to the mature powers of the realm. I am apprentice to the powers put at my disposal. I have youth on my side. I make the mistakes of the inexperienced. When I appear in the guise of the princess I am reminded of my relationship to the forces of queen as consolidator. I too express a stability that has become well established for I represent the fulfilment of idea which will in turn seed a new cycle.

Let us transfer these archetypal characters to the dimensions of ordinary life. Get used to looking for the Tarot Court in everyday life. Here are friends and family, neighbours and colleagues. Try to relate the people you meet in everyday life to the characters at the four courts. The more you observe human nature in the most ordinary circumstances the more you will bring to your interaction with Tarot.

■ Which characters do your work colleagues resemble?
■ Which Tarot character is most like your mother or your father?
■ Which Tarot character do you resemble today?

When laying a spread it is common to choose a court card to represent the questioner. This card is called the significator. It is common to choose kings and queens to represent people over about 35 and to choose knights or pages for younger people. It is also usual to choose a suit which represents their concerns. A young woman seeking advice about a romantic situation might be represented as the Page of Cups. A mature woman asking about a work situation might be represented as the Queen of Discs. When the court cards appear in a reading they are most often taken to be significant people in the life of the querant. For instance the Knight of Swords might be a young man, typically a student, a son, or younger brother. The Page of Wands might be a young man just starting out in life with plenty of enthusiasm and drive. Court cards can also represent ways in which the querant is behaving perhaps even unconsciously. The presence of the Queen of Swords could indicate argumentative or provoking behaviour. The Queen or King of Cups could indicate supportive and caring behaviour. Immature or rash behaviour could be signified by the pages of the various suits. The characters of the Tarot Court show us both sides of the elemental power which is expressed through them. Court cards may fall upright or be reversed. The reversed card – or the dark twin – signifies the negative aspect of the same energy. The reversed meanings indicate the excessive and unstable application of earth, air, fire and water. We see such manifestations in daily life: success turns to greed, love to possessiveness, emotion to sentiment. We have called this the experience of the dark twin which is another archetypal character from world myth and legend. Let us now look at the qualities and characteristics expressed through the Tarot Courts of body, heart, mind and spirit. (You will notice that I refer to the Suit of Discs, but in the Tarot pack we use in this book, this suit is the Pentacles.)

The King of Discs

You will find me seated amid my possessions. My work has brought a rich reward. I now sit and reflect on what I have gained. I have achieved much and gained a great deal. I have created abundance. I am down to earth and practical. I have enjoyed the good life but I am generous too. I have a natural flair for bringing things to increase. I naturally understand what is required of me in the business environment. I give gifts to those I love. I have taken chances and won. Watching my business grow has given me satisfaction and achievement.

A very dark-haired man with dark eyes. Indicates a strong and healthy body with a good character and an excellent mind.

THE KING OF PENTACLES

Caution against gambling or speculation with the possessions of others.

Reversed: I love my possessions. See, I am surrounded by them. I like to look at what I own. I like success and its trappings. I like successful people. I do not want to be reminded of human misery. I like money. I have no qualms about how it may be used or earned. Money makes me feel secure. I think about money a great deal. I think of how I will spend it, but you may be certain I will not spend it on you.

Can you think of a person in your life who is acting as the King of Discs?

The Queen of Discs

You might meet me in the natural surroundings of a garden or out on a long walk. I am often inspired by nature. I am naturally creative and practical. I can turn my hand to almost anything. I am not afraid of a new challenge. I don't mind hard work. I enjoy its rewards. I know what I want in life and I address myself to achieving it. I am trustworthy and responsible. I am sympathetic and constructive, well organised and efficient. I don't waste time or energy. I set myself a goal and do everything in my power to attain it. I am generous to those whom I love and who love me. I enjoy life and its many pleasures and comforts.

Reversed: I am a shadow of what I should have become. My talents are unused. My creativity lies undeveloped. I have failed to find my own confidence and to establish a feeling of security in my natural gifts. I rely on others to make my decisions as I am afraid of shouldering my own responsibilities. I brood over what might have been. Do not rely on me for anything. I cannot help you for I have not learned to help myself.

Can you think of a person in your life who acts as the Queen of Discs?

The Knight of Discs

I offer you the Pentacle of Earth. I understand its meaning for I have integrated its qualities within myself. You will find me hardworking and practical, dependable and patient. I am conscientious and steadfast. Reward comes to me in time. I work hard and reap the reward of my own labours. I plan ahead and work with the future in mind. I do not take risks with what I have. I will share the resources I have gained. I am proud of my achievement.

A very dark-haired, dark-eyed young man. This card indicates new responsibilities.

THE KNIGHT OF PENTACLES

MINOR ARCANA

Be alert or you will miss an important opportunity.

Reversed: I am in love with money and possessions. I delight in the things I can have and own. Others say that possessions have consumed my soul but I have no need for soul so it is irrelevant to me. I am not interested in the ethics of success only in the rewards of success. Beware the effects of a close partnership with me. I will take a short cut and live with the consequences. I am unafraid of big decisions, life is a gamble and I intend to win.

Can you think of a person in your life who is acting as the Knight of Discs?

The Page of Discs

I am the perpetual student with an openness to all life experience. I want to learn from everything and everyone that I meet. I am happy to learn from the experience of others. I am open to advice and practical help. I have my own goals and I am willing to work hard to achieve them. I am creative and enjoy expressing my own ideas. I like to have natural things around me. I find creative inspiration in the natural world.

A very dark-haired, dark-eyed boy or girl. Brings pleasant news.

THE PAGE OF PENTACLES

MINOR ARCANA

Unlucky speculations. Disappointments, losses in friendships. May hear some bad news.

Reversed: I am old before my time because I am already set in my ways. I have set my own furrow and seek no advice from so-called elders, supposed betters or peers. I am not interested in what the past has to show me or what others have to teach me. I am a law unto myself so don't expect me to take any notice of you. Save your breath – I will not be listening.

Can you think of a person in your life who is acting as the Page of Discs?

The King of Swords

I have used the sword of the mind with good effect. I have become a decision-maker. My words are weighed carefully and carry respect and authority. I have used my mental skills to create a professional path in life. I am a good arbitrator. I listen equally well to both sides. I like to debate an issue and take an interest in contemporary life. You will find me unbiased and skilful. I have overcome the obstacles and hardships of life through intelligence and application. I never stop learning. I am open to new ideas and willing to listen to your views. I am diplomatic and trustworthy. I am a good negotiator and a reliable witness.

A dark-haired, brown-eyed man. May be a soldier or a judge, good legal mind.

THE KING OF SWORDS

Use extra care in any matter that could result in a lawsuit.

Reversed: I lack the mental clarity that belongs to my brother. My thinking is confused and muddied. My decision-making is biased and based on prejudice. I use my sword to fight, not to defend. Beware if you seek to cross swords with me. I can plot and plan. I can manipulate and annihilate. You will find me a formidable adversary. I am vindictive and never forget a wrong. I can use the law against you for I like to set a trap and watch you struggle. My advice is not to draw my wrath for once roused I fight to the bitter end.

Can you think of a person in your life who is acting as the King of Swords?

The Queen of Swords

I hold the sword of the mind with pride. I value the freedom that comes from education. I have a mind of my own and say exactly what I mean. I am an independent woman. My mind is sharp and clear. I do not suffer fools gladly. I am direct and outspoken. I say what I mean and mean what I say. I value my own liberty and freedom so do not try to impose your limitations on me. I like to learn and I have many interests. I have gained the respect of others through my respect for truth, fair play and honesty. Come to me for unbiased opinion and fair judgement. Don't seek partisan advice and I won't give it.

A dark-haired, brown-eyed woman; sometimes represents a widow. Indicates loneliness, separation and tears.

THE QUEEN OF SWORDS

A difficult woman to understand. Indicates intolerance and pettiness.

Reversed: My tongue has become my sword. I love to gossip and whatever you say to me in confidence will be used as I see fit. Don't tell me your deepest secret for I will store it up for a future occasion. I love to weave a net of intrigue and half truth, it is so easy to do. I bear old grudges and will bide my time to get even. I sit and brood on the past and all the wrongs done to me. I spend much time planning ways of getting even. I have many opinions and I expect you to agree with them. I am not much interested in you or the greater world at large but only in my own world which I will drag you into like a spider in a web. Beware, you have been warned.

Can you think of a person in your life who is acting as the Queen of Swords?

The Knight of Swords

Look out, I am always in a hurry. I will sweep you off your feet with my plans and projects. My head teems with ideas and possibilities. I am driven by an insatiable curiosity and restless intellectual hunger. I like the excitement that comes from exchanging sharpened words. I like the cut and thrust of debate and intellectual parry. I am confident in my abilities and always acquit myself well. Watch out, I am very persuasive and you might find yourself agreeing with me even when you don't mean to. You will never be bored around me but as soon as I am bored I will move on.

Reversed: Watch out for me. I have mastered the art of mental attack. I will leave you feeling vulnerable and out-manoeuvred. I like to parade my ideas before you and I am not much interested in hearing yours. I have learned to cut to the quick with words. I use humour and wit as a weapon, you cannot defend yourself against me. I will use the whole artillery against you – cynicism, sarcasm and sharp repost are my well-used weapons. If you have any sense just walk away as I intend to win the argument at any cost.

Can you think of a person in your life who is acting as the Knight of Swords?

The Page of Swords

I wield the sword with ease. I am a figure of action. I enjoy the game of life whether mental or physical. I like to compete. I seek out excitement, I bore easily. I like the challenge of the new. I am excited by the possibilities of new developments. I am mentally agile and well informed. I have many interests and an adaptable mind. I can wear you out if you cannot think and act at my pace. I think quickly, I talk quickly. I arrive and depart equally unexpectedly in your life. I am not ready to put down roots. I am still travelling and learning from every experience.

Reversed: I have learned to defend myself with a sharp mind, I will attack you before you have a chance to attack me. You will never feel at ease in my presence, I like to keep you at bay. I am unpredictable and fickle. I am amusing in a cynical and clever way. People like to hear what I have to say but I might say anything to amuse or incite, disrupt or even pacify. I like to argue for its own sake. I will exhaust you into submission. I believe nothing and everything when it suits me.

Can you think of a person in your life who is acting as the Page of Swords?

The King of Wands

People look up to me. I have achieved my ambition. My origins may have been humble but my determination has served me well. I am a self-made man. I do not rest on my laurels. I recognise a new challenge. I am warm and good humoured even with my opponents. I give back to the community at large through my time and effort. I encourage others to believe in themselves and provide as many opportunities as I can. I am devoted and loyal to loved ones and friends. I am honest and generous. I give freely.

Reversed: The fire of my ambition has consumed me. Success has become my goal. I have no time to waste in non-productive effort. I am in charge and I expect others to cede to my demand. I give orders, I do not take them. I know what I want and I will get my way. Other people's feelings are of little consequence. I serve myself first and others not at all.

Can you think of someone in your life who is acting as the King of Wands?

The Queen of Wands

I am the bringer of enthusiasm and energy. You cannot ignore me for my outspokenness will demand your attention. I love nothing more than a heated discussion and I like to play the devil's advocate to see if you can rise to the fray. I mean no harm. I speak my mind and I like you to do the same. I am ambitious for myself and those under my protection. I am good company for I love life and I will draw you into my *joie de vivre*. I have a natural authority and many come for my advice and counsel. I am bold and will bring out your spirit of adventure. I relate easily and spontaneously to everyone. I give warmth and affection. I am creative and original. I am

A blonde woman, possessing a magnetic personality. Success in many undertakings.

THE QUEEN OF WANDS

Deceit and infidelity. A shrew and penny pincher.

popular and confident about myself. I will light the fire of your enthusiasm and give you the confidence to step boldly forward.

Reversed: I have great presence and can use my magnetism to gain what I want. I am ambitious and will use all of my feminine powers to carve my way in the world. Don't stand in my way for I will find a way to remove you. You will find me selfish and bossy, domineering and temperamental. My temper will flare without warning and I am ambitious only for myself. I rise fast in my chosen direction. I am driven by ambition and desire. I have everything it takes to be successful in the world. I play only to win.

Can you think of someone in your life who is acting as the Queen of Wands?

The Knight of Wands

I am the centre of attention without even trying. People always notice me. I have something to contribute wherever I go. I love company and I like to talk and exchange views. I am very active with many interests and projects. I generate enthusiasm wherever I go. I hate being bored. I like to be with people and have fun. I speak my mind directly. I am just myself.

Reversed: I want to be the centre of attention so I will make sure you notice me. I will be controversial to engage you. I will be challenging and confrontational to hold your interest. I have a quick temper too. I am known to throw my weight around to get my own way. You will remember meeting me. You might not look forward to meeting me again.

Can you think of someone in your life who is acting as the Knight of Wands?

The Page of Wands

I express all the youthful energy that cuts a dash and makes itself noticed. I have many new ideas and I thrive on the possibility of change. I am constantly asking questions. I still believe it is possible to change the world. My enthusiasm has not been dulled by harsh reality. I like a challenge and will push myself to achieve a new goal. You will find me refreshing to be with.

Reversed: I will do anything to be noticed. I want to be the centre of attention and will do anything to steal the limelight. I can be temperamental if I don't get what I want, and I want to be seen and heard. My ideas often lack substance but I do not intend to change them one bit. Being outrageous gets me noticed. That is enough.

Can you think of someone in your life who is acting as the Page of Wands?

The King of Cups

I offer you the cup of life. I have drunk deeply
from it myself. I have a deep understanding of
the human condition. I have lived my life with
depth and purpose. I can be your friend or
counsellor, a guiding hand or a shoulder to cry
on. I offer you whatever you need to feel
comforted within yourself. I have a genuine
interest in people. I listen and make time to
hear your needs. I care for everyone I meet
without favour. I help wherever I can.

Reversed: I am a pale reflection of my mature
and grown self. I lack the maturity to act as a
fount of wisdom. I have not lived deeply yet,
but have only skated upon the surface of life
experience. I have not yet learned the meaning of sincerity, instead I use
words to flatter and beguile. I am not to be trusted for my words are for
my own benefit. I have not plumbed the depths of my own being. I do not
know what lies within me.

Can you think of someone in your life who is acting as the King of Cups?

The Queen of Cups

I sit upon my throne looking out to sea where
I find inspiration and wonder. My soul is
nourished by beauty and peace. I dream my
own dreams. I seek harmony and help others
to recognise it. I treasure the gift of loving. I
give myself totally and completely through
love. My inner sensitivity has made me very
aware of the needs of your heart. I will
understand you at a glance and seek to offer
you balm for your wounds. The world is a
harsh place for me. I feel too much in it. I am
content with my chosen company.

Reversed: I have become over-sensitised to the
world and its pain. I wish to escape from the turmoil of life. I have sacrificed
myself for others so often. Others take advantage of my softheartedness. I

escape into my own day dreams where I feel safe. I am overwhelmed by my own feelings. I find fear at every turn. I cannot support you because I have not found my own centre of balance. My world is easily turned upside down.

Can you think of someone in your life who is acting as the Queen of Cups?

The Knight of Cups

I come bearing a chalice like a gift. I have no guile or hidden intentions. I seek to serve all those in need in any way that I can. I seek the best for all around me. I am naturally sensitive. You do not have to explain your needs. I am already attuned to you. I try to show kindness wherever possible. I am idealistic and often take good causes under my wing. I find satisfaction in music, dance, theatre or art. I need to express what I feel and I will help you to do the same.

A young man with light brown hair and hazel eyes. Good news, an invitation to a social affair.

THE KNIGHT OF CUPS

Possible fraud or trickery in connection with a proposition or an offer.

Reversed: I am the bearer of a poisoned chalice. My words are honeyed with false intent. You will hear whatever you need. My charm can steal your heart and I will do this if it suits my purpose. I play with people's emotions. I have not learned any better, so beware. You will find me deeply attractive but I have nothing of substance to offer you.

Can you think of someone in your life who is acting as the Knight of Cups?

The Page of Cups

I bring the openness of youthful love. I have a natural compassion. I am not sharpened by cynicism nor wounded by passion. I offer my simplicity, kindness and sensitivity. I offer a message from the heart or from the invisible world of spirit. I am in touch with psychic levels and speak from my intuition. I am idealistic and believe it is possible to make the world a better place.

A young man or girl with light brown hair and hazel eyes. News or message about the birth of a child.

THE PAGE OF CUPS

Secret or deceptive undertakings will soon be discovered.

Reversed: I gaze into the cup of illusion, it gives me everything I want. I seek to escape from the hard world of fact. I prefer the dream and the fantasy, the short-lived high and the momentary escape. Do not look to me for anything. I do not share your world and you cannot share mine.

Can you think of someone in your life who is acting as the Page of Cups?

The inner courts

We come to Tarot so often for divination that we need to remind ourselves that we may use the same images in a deeper and more personal way. If symbols have the power to create change then selected symbols have the potential to work in particular ways. At a deeper level of involvement the courtly figures bestow the qualities represented in their intrinsic symbolism. If you recognise your need for a compassionate understanding, meditation on the Court of Cups will put you in touch with feelings. If you are undertaking sustained mental or intellectual activity the Court of Swords will serve you. If you are undertaking a new venture meditate on the symbolism of the Court of Discs. If you seek to regain inspiration, meditate on the Court of Wands. Interacting with the characters of the Tarot Courts brings personal response in exactly the same way as all interaction with the symbols of the Tarot. If the pertinent symbolism is absorbed and integrated through meditation it will act like a seed and take root. The cup will become the grail, the wand will become the new backbone. The sword will become the instrument of truth, the disc will become the coinage of the realm. Such images already lie deep within us, we find them in fairy-tale and myth. The hero is given the sword to undertake the quest; the victor drinks from the cup; the bag of coins is given to the youngest son; and the spear of destiny puts the individual in touch with the forces of fate. These are the archetypal constellations that we touch even briefly as we enter the Tarot Court.

The following series of meditations will put you in touch with the essential qualities expressed through the symbolism of the suit. Use the exercises only if you feel a genuine need to develop the powers inherent in the meditation. It is helpful to have the court cards in front of you before you start so that all the details will be clear in your mind. You might like to use the cards for the relevant Tarot Court as a focal point for a general meditation in preparation for these particular encounters. Make notes straight afterwards.

The Court of Discs – the bestowal of the gifts of productivity

This element is associated with the magick of growing things, gardening, farming and animal husbandry and the like, it is also connected with construction, with building and buildings.

Tony Willis, *Magick and the Tarot*

Imagine yourself in a surreal landscape of yellow sky and fertile earth. There is a wonderful scent of rich loam and morning dew. You have come seeking advice in matters of the world. Find yourself approaching the throne of the King of Discs. He is seated on a throne decorated with the symbols of Taurus which signify increase and growth. He wears a robe decorated by the living vine and a crown set with natural symbols. He carries an orb and sceptre. Behind him in the distance you glimpse a castle which is his domain. In your mind, you hear the words 'What do you want from me?' You speak and say clearly what is in your heart and mind. Keep your mind open and you may hear a reply.

Now a softer voice calls your name. You turn and see the throne of the queen where she sits beneath a climbing rose. She holds a pentacle on her lap. As you approach, she lifts it up to show you and remind you of its significance. 'What will you give me?' she asks. You make your reply once again and then spend a few moments in quiet reflection listening for any answer.

Now you hear the stamping of horses' hooves. You turn to see a mounted knight draw back his visor. He reaches into his saddlebag and takes out a pentacle which he holds out as if show you. The horse seems to be growing impatient and you have the feeling the knight is soon to leave on some kind of mission. He asks, 'What shall I bring back to you?' You listen for any reply.

Now you hear a youthful voice singing your name. You turn to see a page of the court – he holds an upraised Pentacle. The Page addresses you directly: 'What will you leave with me in trust for the future?' You think and give an honest reply and wait to hear any further response.

In addressing these four characters you have trodden the circle. Now you turn inwards to face the centre of the circle. Here you find a block of stone on which lies a pentacle. You pick it up and raise it high, saluting each of the courtly figures in turn. When you have finished replace it where you found it for others. Allow the scene to fade and to be utterly dissolved.

The Court of Swords – the bestowal of the gifts of mind

The Suit of Swords stands guardian to the Mysteries of the Path of the intellect. Under its dominion fall all branches of tabulated knowledge and applied science. The Mental Path is the way of logic, wisdom, philosophy and magick.

Tony Willis, *Magick and the Tarot*

Find yourself in an open landscape. The sky is blue. The day is windy and white clouds move across the sky with great rapidity. You have come here to seek counsel in affairs of the mind. You have come seeking the King of Swords. Ahead, you see a figure seated on a throne with a high back of engraved stone. As you approach, you see that he is dressed in a robe of sky blue covered by a cloak of lavender. He is crowned and holds an uplifted sword. The King of Swords addresses you immediately: 'What do you want from me?' You speak and say clearly what is in your heart and mind. Keep your mind open and wait for any reply.

Now a softer voice calls your name. You turn to see the enthroned figure of the queen. Her throne is engraved with a butterfly and a winged cherub, both creatures of the air. She wears a crown of butterflies and a cloak of sky and cloud. She too holds an uplifted sword. 'What will you give me?' she asks. You make your reply. Once again spend time in quiet reflection listening for any reply.

Now you hear the sound of thundering hooves. You turn to see the mounted figure of a knight in armour rushing towards you with sword held aloft. He slows a little as he draws closer. His horse wears a livery decorated with birds and butterflies. 'What shall I bring back to you?' he says. He hardly stops at all. You are left to ponder his question and await an answer.

Now you hear a youthful voice singing your name. A page of the court, simply dressed in lavender tunic and hose, swings a sword with ease. He stands on a small outcrop. 'What will you leave with me in trust for the future?' You contemplate this question and give your answer. Wait on any further reply.

In addressing these four characters you have trodden the circle. Now you turn inwards to face the centre of the circle. Here you find a block of stone on which lies a sword. You pick it up and raise it high, saluting each of the courtly figures in turn. When you have finished replace it where you found it for others. Allow the scene to fade. Dissolve all the images you have created.

The Court of Wands – the bestowal of the gifts of spiritual fire

Self-confidence is the key to success in the public eye, for self confidence encourages the growth of leadership and management skills and executive ability. The Mysteries of the Suit of Wands are to do with the development, strengthening and drawing out of the qualities.

Tony Willis, *Magick and the Tarot*

Imagine yourself in a hot dry landscape. The sky is a brilliant blue. Everywhere you see the yellow of desert sand and in the distance you see the familiar outline of pyramids. The air is already hot. You have come seeking advice for yourself. Find yourself approaching the throne of the King of Wands. He is seated on a throne decorated with the symbols of the lion. A lizard scuttles at his feet. He is clothed in the hot colours of yellow and orange and wears a golden crown. He holds a wand burgeoning with new shoots. In your mind, you hear the words, 'What do you want from me?' You speak and clearly explain what is in your heart and mind. Keep your mind open and you may hear a reply.

Now a softer voice calls your name. You turn and see another throne. Directly ahead of you a woman sits on a throne decorated and supported by lions. In one hand she holds a sunflower and in the other the upright wand which signifies the power of this domain. A black cat sits in front of her throne. 'What will you give me?' she asks. You make your reply once again and then spend a few moments in quiet reflection listening for any answer.

Now you hear the stamping of horses' hooves. You turn to see a mounted knight on a rearing horse. Over his armour he wears a tunic of yellow decorated with heraldic signs. He wields the wand in one hand while controlling the horse beneath him with the other. He asks you, 'What shall I bring back to you?' You listen for any reply.

Now you hear a youthful voice singing your name. You turn to see a page of the court standing with a single rod of wood. He too is dressed in the colours of this court, yellow and orange decorated with heraldic symbols. The page addresses you directly: 'What will you leave with me in trust for the future?' You think and give an honest reply and wait to hear any further response.

In addressing these four characters you have trodden the circle. Now you turn inwards to face the centre of the circle. Here you see a tripod supporting a brazier where a small fire burns. At the edge of the brazier you see a taper cut from wood. You light the taper and it catches straight away. You raise it on high, saluting each of the courtly figures in turn. Place the last piece in the brazier and watch it burn. Allow the scene to fade. Then dissolve the images completely.

The Court of Cups – the bestowal of the gifts of the heart

> The Suit of Cups and the Physical Path are concerned with love, the affections and the emotions. The Mysteries of this Path are those of the planet Venus and to a lesser extent the moon.
>
> Tony Willis, *Magick and the Tarot*

Imagine yourself at the shoreline. There is a wonderful scent of salt water and the sound of rolling waves. You have come seeking advice in matters of the heart. Find yourself approaching the throne of the King of Cups. He is seated on a throne set upon a block in shallow water. To reach him you will have to get your feet wet. He holds a chalice in one hand and a lotus wand in the other. Behind him in the distance you see a turtle and in the far distance you glimpse a ship. In your mind, you hear the words 'What do you want from me?' You speak and say clearly what is in your heart and mind. Keep your mind open and you may hear a reply.

Now a softer voice calls your name. You turn and see the throne of the queen. It is set right at the edge where land and water meet. Pebbles and shells are massed around her feet and in both hands she holds an ornate covered chalice. 'What will you give me?' she asks. You make your reply once again and then spend a few moments in quiet reflection listening for any answer.

Now you hear the stamping of horses' hooves. You turn to see a mounted knight on a pale horse. He wears the livery of this court. He extends a chalice to you.You sense that he is waiting to leave. He asks you, 'What shall I bring back to you?' You listen for any reply.

Now you hear a youthful voice singing your name. You turn to see a page of the court holding a chalice. Unexpectedly a fish is bobbing up from within. The page addresses you directly: 'What will you leave with me in trust for the future?' You think and give an honest reply and wait to hear any further response.

In addressing these four characters you have trodden the circle. Now you turn inwards to face the centre of the circle. Here you will find a table inset with seashells and stones from the sea. In the centre is a beautiful chalice inscribed with water signs. You pick it up and drink deeply. The water is rich in minerals and you feel invigorated by it. Finally you raise it on high, saluting each of the courtly figures in turn. When you have finished replace the chalice where you found it. Allow the scene to fade and finally to be dissolved completely.

If you find that these meditations serve as triggers for events and changes in everyday life, you will have come to personally discover the curious reflective relationship of inner psyche and outer reality.

Summary

- You have encountered the Tarot Courts as a voice for divination.
- You have encountered the Tarot Courts as a voice for personal development.

6 THE FOUR ORACLES

To the Ancients, the number four held great significance. It symbolised wholeness and completion.

Tony Willis, *Magick and the Tarot*

The Four Oracles and the Tree of Life

We have already met the Cup, Sword, Rod (Wand) and Pentacle (Disc) through The Magician. We have looked at the elemental symbolism of earth, air, fire and water. We have gained an overview of the significance of each of the four suits. We have looked at the elemental Tarot courts. Let us now look at the four suits in their oracular capacity.

You will surely have guessed by now that the Minor Arcana cards have a particular relationship with the Tree of Life. We will use this as our starting point as it provides an intellectual structure which we can use as a springboard for the intuition. The Tree is represented through the ten Sephiroth and four worlds, the Archetypal World symbolised by 'Yod', the World of Creation symbolised by 'He', the World of Formation symbolised by 'Vau' and the World of Action symbolised by the 'He final'. The numbered suits of the Tarot provide ten cards in each of the four suits. The match is too tempting to ignore. The Tarot and the Tree of Life just seem to be made for each other. Each of the numbered cards is assigned to its related numbered Sephiroth, the twos are assigned to the second Sephirah, the threes to the third, and so on. The way the pip cards are placed on the Tree symbolises the descent of spiritual force into material form. The aces are referred to as the Roots of the Powers of the suit. Assigning the aces to Kether serves to symbolise their creative essence. The tens represent the most concrete aspect of each suit. In between, ace and ten, cards and Sephiroth meet. The Sephiroth express certain characteristics and functions and the card brings its own elemental nature too. This resulting marriage of energies may prove to be co-operative, antagonistic, even on occasion excessive. Let us see how this relationship serves to deepen the meaning of each card. The numbered cards are allocated to the Tree of Life in the following way (see Figure 6.1).

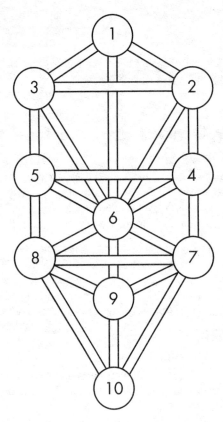

1 Kether – The Crown – the four Aces
2 Chokmah – Wisdom – the four Twos
3 Binah – the four Threes
4 Chesed – Mercy the four Fours
5 Geburah – the four Fives

6 Tiphareth – the four Sixes
7 Netzach – the four Sevens
8 Hod – the four Eights
9 Yesod – the four Nines
10 Malkuth – the four Tens

Figure 6.1   The numbered cards and the Tree of Life

The Four Aces in Kether

Kether represents unity. It represents the source of all that was and is and will be. The Aces are called the Roots of the Powers of their respective suits. Each symbolises a beginning:

- The Ace of Discs suggests the beginning of a practical project.
- The Ace of Swords suggests a new and important idea.
- The Ace of Wands suggests the beginning of a creative or artistic project.
- The Ace of Cups suggests a new beginning in love.

The Four Twos in Chokmah

Chokmah introduces the first duality. Here is the archetypal yang energy. We see the dynamic quest for equilibrium in the twos:

- The Two of Discs depicts the flow in the affairs of the world.
- The Two of Swords depicts the weighing of one possibility against another.
- The Two of Wands depicts the weighing of possible outcomes.
- The Two of Cups depicts a harmonious balance.

The Four Threes in Binah

Binah is the place of growth. Here is the archetypal feminine yin energy which receives earth, water, fire well enough, but here the sword destroys:

- The Three of Discs shows growth from hard work, application and labour.
- The Three of Swords shows the destruction of growth.
- The Three of Wands shows potential growth which is not yet complete.
- The Three of Cups shows personal emotional growth.

The Four Fours in Chesed

Chesed is the sphere of Mercy which is expressed through stability. The fours interpret the theme of stability in accordance with the energies of the suit:

- The Four of Discs shows financial success which is often the basis of stability.
- The Four of Swords shows personal recuperation as a means of restoring mental stability.
- The Four of Wands shows celebration which can only be enjoyed when stable circumstances prevail.
- The Four of Cups shows the inner soul searching which arises when emotional stability has become a little too settled and predictable.

The Four Fives in Geburah

Geburah represents the process of breakdown and disintegration. This theme is expressed through all the fives:

- The Five of Discs shows a scene of poverty.
- The Five of Swords shows the aftermath of a skirmish.
- The Five of Wands shows conflict.
- The Five of Cups shows a scene of despair.

The Four Sixes in Tiphareth

Tiphareth is called Beauty or Harmony. The theme of harmony restored runs through all of the sixes:

- The Six of Discs shows the distribution of largesse.
- The Six of Swords shows a journey away from difficulty.
- The Six of Wands shows the celebration of victory.
- The Six of Cups shows a cheerful homecoming.

The Four Sevens in Netzach

Netzach represents the emotional nature which can be unstable if not balanced by a clear mind:

- The Seven of Discs shows us discontent.
- The Seven of Swords shows us self-sabotage.
- The Seven of Wands shows us confrontation.
- The Seven of Cups shows us emotional confusion.

The Four Eights in Hod

Hod represents the intellectual mind which can be dry without the balancing effect of feeling and imagination.

- The Eight of Discs shows us an industrious and active scene which results from the practical application of an idea.
- The Eight of Swords shows us the imprisonment which comes from rigid mental attitudes.
- The Eight of Wands shows us the return of mental clarity.
- The Eight of Cups shows us dissatisfaction at life devoid of emotional warmth.

The Four Nines in Yesod

Yesod symbolises the unconscious and psychic realm. It is a storehouse of much creativity.

- The Nine of Discs shows us the benefits which follow daily activities and reflect deep-seated feelings.
- The Nine of Swords shows us the conflict which arises when the analytical mind attempts to ignore, diminish or over-intellectualise a realm that defies analysis.
- The Nine of Wands shows us the defensive stance which arises when willpower attempts to override feelings.
- The Nine of Cups shows us a positive blend as feelings and deep-seated needs meet.

The Four Tens in Malkuth

Malkuth represents the physical world as it appears to our senses.

- The Ten of Discs shows us the positive results which accrue from utilising all the active qualities expressed through the element of earth.
- The Ten of Swords shows us how the mind is constrained and rendered invisible in this sphere of worldly experience. The ensuing feeling is one of entrapment and isolation.
- The Ten of Wands shows us how the responsibilities of the world are often experienced as burdens. The element of fire naturally seeks freedom.

■ The Ten of Cups shows us that the element of water feels comfortable and able to find expression in this physical realm.

The Minor Arcana also carry astrological correspondences and titles. These attributions further add to the meaning of the cards and serve as a shorthand.

The Suit of Discs

1   The Root of the Powers of Earth.
2   Change – Jupiter in Capricorn.
3   Work – Mars in Capricorn.
4   Power – Sun in Capricorn.
5   Worry – Venus in Taurus.
6   Success – Moon in Taurus.
7   Failure – Saturn in Taurus.
8   Prudence – Sun in Virgo.
9   Gain – Venus in Virgo.
10 Wealth – Mercury in Virgo.

The Suit of Swords

1   The Root of the Powers of Air.
2   Peace – Moon in Libra.
3   Sorrow – Saturn in Libra.
4   Truce – Jupiter in Libra.
5   Defeat – Venus in Aquarius.
6   Science – Mercury in Aquarius.
7   Futility – Moon in Gemini.
8   Interference – Jupiter in Gemini.
9   Cruelty – Mars in Gemini.
10 Ruin – Sun in Gemini.

The Suit of Wands

1   The Root of the Powers of Fire.
2   Dominion – Mars in Aries.
3   Virtue – Moon in Aries.

4   Completion – Venus in Aries.
5   Strife – Saturn in Leo.
6   Victory – Jupiter in Leo.
7   Valour – Mars in Leo.
8   Swiftness – Mercury in Sagittarius.
9   Strength – Moon in Sagittarius.
10   Oppression – Saturn in Sagittarius.

The Suit of Cups

1   The Roots of the Powers of Water.
2   Love – Venus in Cancer.
3   Abundance – Mercury in Cancer.
4   Luxury – Moon in Cancer.
5   Disappointment – Mars in Scorpio.
6   Pleasure – Sun in Scorpio.
7   Debauch – Venus in Scorpio.
8   Indolence – Saturn in Pisces.
9   Happiness – Jupiter in Pisces.
10   Satiety – Mars in Pisces.

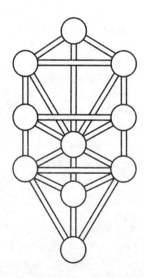

Figure 6.2   The template of the Tree of Life

Now take the template of the Tree of Life (see Figure 6.2) and place each of the pip cards in the appropriate Sephirah. Do this for each of the suits in turn. This relationship between the Tarot and the Tree provides a firm foundation for exploring the numbered cards in depth. Although working directly with the visual symbolism of the Tarot is an excellent way of remembering the scene and creating your own set of meanings, not every Tarot pack provides as much visual information as, for example, the Rider-Waite deck. We may therefore profitably draw upon this structure of the Tree as an additional *aide-mémoire*. Let us combine what we already know and approach the symbolism of the suits directly. We will begin with the aces which hold the key symbolism of the suit. Have the four aces in front of you. Take each of the main symbols in turn and make a list of all the associations and connections that spring to mind.

- Look at the symbolism of the Disc: what does this mean to you?
- Look at the symbolism of the Sword: what does this mean to you?
- Look at the symbolism of the Cup: what does this mean to you?
- Look at the symbolism of the Wand or Rod: what does this mean to you?

This process of association will lead you to make other connections. The more associations that you understand and internalise, the more you will be able to bring to your work with the Tarot. Next take each of the Aces in turn and look at the specific images which are presented to you. What do these individual cards say to you? Have the cards in front of you. Just look at them and write down whatever comes to mind. Also use the astrological information if you are able.

- Look at the Ace of Swords: you see an upraised sword held in a strong hand. A crown is magically suspended around the tip of the sword. Six golden droplets hang in the air. Two kinds of greenery hang from the crown. What does this scene say to you?
- Look at the Ace of Wands: you see an upraised baton sprouting with new growth. Beneath you see a castle set on a hilly outcrop. What does this scene say to you?

■ The Ace of Cups: you see a chalice spouting four streams. A dove is descending into the chalice bearing a wafer. Beneath we see waters bearing lotus blooms. What does this scene say to you?

■ The Ace of Discs: you see a cupped hand holding a disc inscribed with a five-pointed star. Beneath you see an arbour of roses. What does this scene say to you?

This initial approach to the key symbols of each suit is designed to start you thinking deeply about these images. When you feel confident that you have gathered a broad range of associations move on to internalise these associations and ideas. Enter a relaxed and meditative state and re-create the image on the card while allowing your mind to dwell on all the associations and ideas that you have already generated. If new ideas or realisations come to you, note them and follow them up later. When the key symbols of the suits have become internalised, you might wish to take your explorations to an even deeper level of meaning. These key images have been linked to archetypal mythological symbols. Look into the reservoirs of mythology where you will find recurring images of the Sword of Truth, the Cup of Love, the Rod of Power and the Coin of Abundance. Let these stories guide, inspire and enrich you, if you so wish.

The suits in more detail

As the aces have been referred to as the Roots of the Powers of each suit, we have begun by establishing these roots firmly in the ground of the mind. Now let us approach the suit itself using both the intellect and the intuition. Compile your own notes before cross-referencing your ideas with those from books. If you simply rely on the ideas given by others you will always be trying to memorise them and will not develop the confidence to draw on your own. Make your own notes on these brief vignettes of life. The numbered cards like the court cards may also be read as reversed when they fall upside down. So look at each of the cards in this light. Have the four suits ready. Arrange the suits by number so that you have groups of twos, threes, etc.

■ Take each of the sets in turn. Apply the principles of examination, observation and free association.

■ What do you see taking place in each card? Invent your own storyboard. What has just happened in the Tarot snapshot? What will happen next in your imaginary scenario?

We will look at the suits as a unity by summarising all we have learned through the elemental and astrological symbolism, the relationship to the Tree of Life and the direct visual symbolism of the card itself. It is important to note that these meanings are not definitive, merely suggestive. The work and study which leads you to find your own meanings carries more value.

Suit of Discs

When working with the Suit of Discs, keywords are: fertility, resources and values, bank balance, property and possessions, valuables, business, money and savings, outgoings, security, increment, growth, status, practical application, manufacture, craftsmanship, construction, using natural resources. Also, remember that some packs call these cards Pentacles.

The Oracle of the Suit of Discs – Ace of Discs

The Root of the Powers of Earth

A tangible improvement – a new possibility, perhaps a new job prospect – maybe even a win, windfall or an unexpected bonus.

Reversed: Forthcoming money is delayed.

The card of good fortune. This card greatly improves the fortune of the cards around it.

THE ACE OF PENTACLES

Undeserved riches that come with corruption.

Ability to make successful changes with very little opposition.

THE TWO OF PENTACLES

Messages or letters that are very controversial.

Two of Discs

Change – Jupiter in Capricorn

I show you the ups and downs in life, having to juggle money carefully to get by. Perhaps this indicates an unexpected change of plans, direction or circumstances. Be flexible, go with the flow.

Reversed: Change feels uncomfortable and difficult. Could be the break-up of a partnership and a division of resources.

Three of Discs

Work – Mars in Capricorn

I show you the results of hard work, the opportunity to show what you can do. The labourer is rewarded, hard work, talent and application are paying off. Achievement in one's chosen career.

Reversed: Shoddy work and insufficient application brings only meagre recognition.

Four of Discs

Power – Sun in Capricorn

I show you a man rooted in his work and reward. Here is economic and financial stability. But don't be too possessive about what you have.

Reversed: Control seems to evade you. Financial insecurity – money slips through your fingers.

Five of Discs

Worry – Venus in Taurus

I show you a scene of Victorian poverty and loss – possibly unemployment or redundancy, loss of income and sudden change of expectation. Here is much uncertainty and anxiety – feeling left out. Health issues may be relevant too.

Reversed: There is a light at the end of the tunnel. Something or someone has restored your faith in human nature and yourself.

Six of Discs

Success – Moon in Taurus

I show you success – a time for reaping financial rewards, investments pay out – dividends have multiplied. A time to pay off debts and repay favours. A time to share with others. You can afford to be charitable.

Reversed: An expected and deserved bonus does not appear.

Seven of Discs

Failure – Saturn in Taurus

I show you a man regarding what he has gained from life. There is a sense of failure and disappointment. The harvest no longer seems worth the effort demanded or values have changed. Work no longer seems satisfying.

Reversed: The harvest has become a burden – worries about mortgages, financial repayments, etc. A general disillusionment with life.

Eight of Discs

Prudence – Sun in Virgo

I show you an industrious soul hard at work, the determination to improve one's situation through practical steps. Perhaps learning a new skill or seeking a new qualification.

Reversed: Maybe a wish to short circuit the system by quick and even underhand means.

Nine of Discs

Gain – Venus in Virgo

I show you a woman admiring the garden which she once planted. It has now come to fruition. It has grown through wise cultivation, wisdom has been applied. Care has been taken in the past.

Reversed: The unkempt garden will be full of weeds. Foolish moves, rash decisions and lack of foresight in the past now bring the only possible harvest.

Your well-being is assured by your successful accomplishments.

THE NINE OF PENTACLES

Bad faith and disappointment may result in the loss of important friendships.

A good card for real estate investments. Indicates prosperity in family affairs.

THE TEN OF PENTACLES

Loss of legacy. Misfortune in the family. Avoid gambling.

Ten of Discs

Wealth – Mercury in Virgo

I show you stability, money, security and success – reaping the rewards of much hard work, perhaps a pension pay out or salary increase. Also the possibility of a positive transition from single to married or employed to retired.

Reversed: Security is in doubt – a reputation is in jeopardy. Dealing with big business is fraught with problems. Big financial decisions are unstable. It feels as if circumstances conspire against our best wishes.

Suit of Swords

When working with the Suit of Swords, keywords are: ideas, worries, serious decisions, delays, disappointments, losses, separations, matters which require a specialist, travel, movement, ambition, enthusiasm, excitement, courage, enterprise, restlessness, impulsiveness, recklessness.

The Oracle of the Suit of Swords – Ace of Swords

A powerful card. Materially helps the cards surrounding it.

THE ACE OF SWORDS

Brings disaster to the cards around it.

The Root of the Powers of Air

The emergence of a powerful idea or a plan, scheme or possibility.

Reversed: Keep a sense of proportion about your sense of power. Don't antagonise others.

Indicates better understanding of family problems. Possible reconciliation.

THE TWO OF SWORDS

Beware of strangers carrying gifts. Check offerings carefully.

Two of Swords

Peace – Moon in Libra

I show you the weighing of one possibility against another. Here is indecision for the scales seem perfectly balanced – possibly even an agreement to defer a solution or decision until the future.

Reversed: A decision has been taken – change will follow.

Three of Swords

Sorrow – Saturn in Libra

I show you the pierced heart wounded by cruel words – heartache. A time for endings. Bitter words have caused much pain. May also indicate physical heart problems.

Reversed: Separation and loss. The beginning of recovery. Is there something to be learned about yourself from this?

The loss of a lover. Sorrow and disappointments.

THE THREE OF SWORDS

Great disillusionment. Disorder and confusion.

Four of Swords

Truce – Jupiter in Libra

I show you a knight in repose. It is a time for recuperation, or retreat. Perhaps a vacation is needed. A period of mental rest would be beneficial. Possibly a connection with hospitals as a place of rest and recovery.

Reversed: Renewed action is possible. A return to the fray with recharged batteries and restored energy.

Five of Swords

Defeat – Venus in Aquarius

I show you a time of tension and unpleasantness. Cruel words are in the air. Revenge and gamesmanship are the order of the day. Someone will get hurt in this battle of words. Watch out for underhand dealing.

Reversed: Little improvement. But who is the victim? Something will be lost or broken, someone's pride perhaps!

Six of Swords

Science – Mercury in Aquarius

I show you movement away from the past to new possibilities. Either a new attitude or new location will put distance between you and any difficulties.

Reversed: You cannot move away either mentally or physically – stalemate.

Seven of Swords

Futility – Moon in Gemini

I show you stealth and trickery, cunning and underhand dealing. Who is stealing from you? Who is taking what is not theirs – perhaps your good name and reputation? Who is stealing your thunder or taking credit for your ideas?

Reversed: The situation has been righted with an apology or an admission of fault – that which is rightfully yours is returned.

Eight of Swords

Interference – Jupiter in Gemini

I show you imprisonment. I show you the mental anguish of feeling trapped by a situation, a person or a circumstance. A difficult situation, perhaps a young mother trapped by circumstance. There is a great desire to be free.

Reversed: You see the way out and cut yourself free through your own ideas and initiative.

Nine of Swords

Cruelty – Mars in Gemini

I show you despair, the moment of waking in the night from tormented sleep. All around seems dark. Is there no escape? Possibility of health issues too.

Reversed: There is light at the end of the tunnel, nothing lasts for ever.

Ten of Swords

Ruin – Sun in Gemini

I show you what feels like ultimate defeat and catastrophe. The end has arrived – the battle has been lost – a stab in the back.

Reversed: In every ending there is new beginning. It is time too for a total re-evaluation of what you have been trying to accomplish. It is time to lick your wounds and look towards the future.

Suit of Wands

When working with the Suit of Wands, keywords are: energy, enthusiasm, communications, letters, phone calls, distant travel, enterprise, business concerns, negotiations.

The Oracle of the Suit of Wands – Ace of Wands

The Roots of the Powers of Fire

I show you a positive beginning, a new opportunity and creative challenge.

Reversed: You will be keen to make a start but delays and obstacles will appear.

Two of Wands

Dominion – Mars in Aries

I show you a man thinking about business. He has created some success and wonders whether to act in the present or await on news. Partner or others may be involved. This is a good time to act.

Reversed: I show you hope and anticipation. The man waits with a sense of expectancy and eagerness but he has not acted and the hoped for goal is likely to fade on the horizon. Delays are indicated.

Three of Wands

Virtue – Sun in Aries

I show you a man looking towards the horizon once more. Ships are returning home, good news is likely. Travel in connection with work is on the horizon. Teamwork and co-operation have paid off.

Reversed: I show you a man looking in vain towards the same horizon. The ships will land elsewhere, the expected opportunity does not transpire.

Four of Wands

Completion – Venus in Aries

I show you success and delight, celebration and satisfaction. There is something real to celebrate – perhaps a new house, putting down roots or marking an anniversary.

Reversed: Nothing can spoil the day. The spirit of celebration is genuine.

Five of Wands

Strife – Saturn in Leo

I show you struggle and argument at home or at work. Rivals engage in power games, opinions are divided. Who will win the day? Delay or misunderstood communication is likely. A sense of challenge.

Reversed: The battle is over, perhaps a reorganisation has taken place.

Six of Wands

Victory – Jupiter in Leo

I show you victory after much effort – a well earned success, a triumphant return or successful outcome to a dispute or negotiation.

Reversed: Take care – the victory that you have expected may go elsewhere.

Seven of Wands

Valour – Mars in Leo

I show you a man defending his position. He fights for his beliefs and values. The situation is coming to a head. Problems pop up in every direction. Try to tackle them one at a time.

Reversed: The immediate situation is defused. Tensions exist but do not surface, an uneasy and probably temporary solution.

Eight of Wands

Swiftness – Mercury in Sagittarius

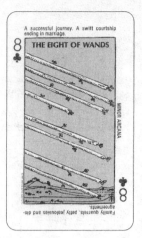

I show you a volley of wands travelling at speed. The action around you is fast moving and skilful. Your ideas will rapidly become real. Success and skill are indicated. Travel may be indicated.

Reversed: Your ideas may fall flat before reaching their intended mark.

Nine of Wands

Strength – Moon in Sagittarius

I show you a man on guard. He looks tense from watchfulness and expectancy. He is already wounded but he prepares to fight again if necessary. Health problems may be indicated.

Reversed: The battle has been won. Vigilance is required but the real action is over.

Ten of Wands

Oppression – Saturn in Sagittarius

I show you a man weighed down with the weight of responsibilities and burdens that he has to shoulder. He is carrying a great deal single-handed. Over-commitment stretches mind and body. Try to delegate or otherwise share the weight with others.

Reversed: I show you a man not looking where he is going. The weight of the burden blinds him to real purpose and direction. Care is required or he will fall or trip under its weight. Health problems may be indicated.

Suit of Cups

When working with the Suit of Cups, keywords are: feelings, depth, emotion, sensitivity, relationship, compassion, caring, love, comfort, friendship, companionship, colleagues, creativity, activities, fulfilment, celebration, desolation, romance, surprise.

The Oracle of the Suit of Cups – Ace of Cups

The Roots of the Powers of Water

I show you a positive beginning – a new friendship or supportive work association – love and friendship, even the possibility of romance. A good social life.

Reversed: You will be keen to make new friends or just get out more, but delays and obstacles will appear to thwart your hopes.

Very favorable card. Indicates love, happiness and abundance.

THE ACE OF CUPS

A reversal in your present state of affairs. Uncertainty.

A new romance or friendship. Cooperation in partnership affairs.

THE TWO OF CUPS

False promises, instability in emotional matters.

Two of Cups

Love – Venus in Cancer

I show you reciprocal exchange of love. Here is harmony and peace. Here is accord and joy.

Reversed: I show the failure of love, infatuation has worn off – the parting of the ways or an ending of a friendship.

Three of Cups

Abundance – Mercury in Cancer

The card of friendship, good for parties, health. Signifies the horn of plenty.

I show you delight and joy. The girls dance with joyful exuberance. Here is celebration, a time for friends, family and loved ones – a party perhaps – possible connections to a wedding.

Reversed: I show you that you can have too much of a good thing. Take care, don't overdo the good time as you will regret the indulgence afterwards.

A fall or accident. Avoid physical and emotional excess.

A desire for a change that should be carefully considered. Indecision about a new venture.

A change in your present plans. A new association that will prove troublesome.

Four of Cups

Luxury – Moon in Cancer

I show you a thoughtful person taking the time to reflect on life. Something new is being offered. This is not the time to make a rushed decision. It is time to look at what is really important.

Reversed: The time for reflection has passed. Now is the time to re-emerge and take up the reins again.

Five of Cups

Disappointment – Mars in Scorpio

I show you disappointment, grieving for what might have been and for what has been lost.

Reversed: Time heals. Nurture the spark of hope and set out again.

Disappointment in marriage or an inheritance.

News from an old friend. A new business proposition.

Six of Cups

Pleasure – Sun in Scorpio

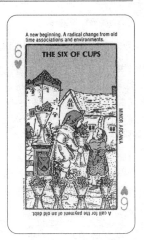

I show you the pleasure of memory and the celebration of significant dates and events, perhaps the renewal of a friendship from the past. A spark from the past might flicker into new life.

Reversed: Let go of the past and move into the present. A time to get a perspective on childhood memories.

Seven of Cups

Debauch – Venus in Scorpio

I show you the confusion that comes from too many choices. Everything seems tempting but you are pulled in different directions – not a time to make a decision.

Reversed: Clarity has dawned, you know which cup you will choose.

Eight of Cups

Indolence – Saturn in Pisces

I show you a sad man turning his back on the work of the past. He just walks away. Now he looks for something more meaningful.

Reversed: Walking away has created a new possibility. Involvement in meaningful activity is close at hand.

Nine of Cups

Happiness – Jupiter in Pisces

Good health, honor and financial gains.

THE NINE OF CUPS

Guard against over-indulgence in both food
and drink. Liable to mistakes in judgment.

I show you a contented man. He looks relaxed and at ease. He is enjoying what he has already worked for. There is time for socialising and enjoyment. Life is enjoyable at the moment. A time to count one's blessings.

Reversed: The temptations of ease and success beckon. Take care, indulgence feels good only in the short run.

Your wish comes true. Success and happiness in the family circle.

THE TEN OF CUPS

The loss of a close friend. Family quarrels and upsets.

Ten of Cups

Satiety – Mars in Pisces

I show you a vision of contentment. Here is happiness and fulfilment in relationships and especially at home. Here is harmony and joy. The rainbow signifies hope for tomorrow.

Reversed: The situation will not last, happiness is fleeting. Perhaps someone is leaving home.

Summary

- You have seen how the pip cards of the Minor Arcana relate to the Tree of Life as an intellectual structure.
- You have looked at the symbolism of the pip cards directly.
- You have looked at the pip cards as the oracular voice of the elemental suit.

7 | THE MAJOR ARCANA

The Major Arcana represents the Way of the Hero in each of us.
Karen Hamaker-Zondag, *Tarot as a Way of Life*

The Journey of the Fool

The Trumps or Triumphs of the Major Arcana are often described as the Journey of the Fool. Here we meet and encounter the archetypal forces of life through the imagery and symbolism assigned to each Trump. The Trumps can be approached in a variety of ways and patterns. The classic journey follows the sequence from the first card of the Fool to the final card of the World. Qabalistically the sequence is approached in reverse order beginning with the World and finishing with the Fool. Each of the Trumps is assigned to a Path on the Tree. The Paths are traditionally travelled and internalised in a particular order. Putting the Tree to one side, the Trumps may be simply approached individually. You might for instance choose a Trump at random, or spread out the pack and select one that strongly attracts or even repels you. You can use this as a focal point for study and meditation until you are ready to move on to another. First assess your own understanding of the Major Arcana. Are you familiar with the names, numbering and order? Can you call the visual details of each Trump to mind with clarity? Are you familiar with the symbolism and correspondences of each Trump? Work first to secure your intellectual foundation. Deepen your understanding through meditation and visualisation. The Tarot itself will teach you. Anticipate future rewards such as creativity, insight and inspiration.

The following series of meditations are at your disposal. The meditations may be used in a variety of ways. Break the journey into as many or as few sections as you wish. Put the readings on tape or speak them aloud. Have the relevant Trumps before you as you proceed with this journey.

Take as much time as you need. Each reading is an evocation which is designed to bring you closer to an aspect of yourself and your life. At the end of your meditation write up any thoughts or insights. These are the fruits of your journey.

Evocation of the Fool, Tarot Trump 0

I am known as the Fool. I am the Fool who is as yet without knowledge or experience. Like a child I step out into life eager for experience and possibility. My journey begins here and now in this moment. See the abyss at my feet. My next step shall carry me forwards and downwards. I have a good companion for the journey too. My instinctive response will stand me in good stead. I face towards the future as I step out from the place of the Divine Source. Look at my face, I am neither male nor female for I encompass the totality of your being. I carry all that I need in the pouch which bears the sign of the eagle. This is the badge of Scorpio which is the power of  transformation. I too will be transformed on my journey. My number is 0, the No-Thing from which all things come and return. This zero does not signify an emptiness but potentiality. See my robe. I wear the white inner robe of my true self. It is already masked by my outer garment. My outer robe is black which is the colour attributed to Saturn, the bringer of time and boundary. But I do not forget my spiritual identity. See the decorations upon my robe. Here is the Tree of Life in another form. It is here to remind me. At my heart I bear a triple flame within a yellow circle. Close to the hem of my robe, I bear the sign of Shin which is elemental fire, which is Spirit itself. I uphold the white rose as a symbol of perfection, beauty and innocence. I am your power to begin anew. I am your power to be transformed by every experience. If you see me in a spread, I am your ability to undertake the new and the adventurous, to set out again and again. I am your willingness to act spontaneously with childlike joy, to step forward with hope and openness. I am the Fool in you.

Evocation of the Magician, Tarot Trump I

I am the Magician. Here I stand at the table of the elements. Here are the representations of my own being: earth, air, fire and water. I am represented here as physical body, emotional body, mental body and soul body. I acknowledge myself in these symbols. See the Sword, Rod, Cup and Pentacle. I see myself reflected here. I offer you the gift of the elements too. I am crowned with a circlet of gold for I am awake to the powers of my whole being. See the sign of infinity above my head. My becoming is an endless cycle set in infinity. Like the serpent around my waist, I become myself as I consciously slough off the outworn. I wear the red and the white, body and soul. See that I stand amidst roses and lilies. Cultivated from the wild five-petalled flower, the rose shows evolution and draws me back to the sign of the five-pointed star which is the sign of the microcosm, the world below. The lily has six petals, in cross-section I see a six-pointed star which is the sign of the macrocosm, the world above. In recognition of the duality of creation I lift one hand to the heavens, the other points down into the world. I understand the connection between the greater and lesser worlds. I remember the Hermetic phrase, 'As Above so Below'. I remember and honour the ancient wisdom which is eternal and timeless, I see its application in daily life. I will become a living bridge between the two worlds of the seen and the unseen. I will take the responsibility for constructing myself. I express the desire for self-mastery and self-knowledge. With these tools I will become the person I was intended to be. I am your power to bring things to pass, to act decisively and in accordance with the greater laws. I affirm your desire for self-mastery and self-understanding. If you see me in a spread, I am your ability to act consciously and win alignment with wisdom. I am the Magician in you.

Evocation of the High Priestess, Tarot Trump II

I am the High Priestess. Welcome to the temple within. This place is open to all who seek the inner life of the soul with true intent. I hold the book of life in my lap. Is it your wish to know what is written here in the scroll

of law? What will you do with such
knowledge? Do not mistake knowledge for
gnosis. Only gnosis can nourish the soul. If
you seek me, I will bring you to wisdom. I
dwell within the Temple of the Mysteries of
Being and Becoming. I sit between the pillars
of life, the eternal polarities which emerge
from the one. My number is two which is the
dynamic polarity of manifestation. See the veil
at my back which is decorated with
pomegranates, the many seeded fruit of the
Goddess. Glimpse beyond the veil at my back.
See the vast ocean. It is whole of itself, virgin
perfection. It is the universal energy beneath
and within all life. It is the great ocean, eternal

life itself. I serve the Ancient Wisdom. I uphold the light of the Mysteries.
This is my domain, the holy temple of being and becoming and I am the
servant upon the throne. I am the eternal servant of the Great Goddess
whose names are without number. Where She is I am to be found and She
is to be found at all times and in all places whether secretly or openly. This
is her temple and I am her servant. My inner mind has been opened and
awakened to the invisible realms. My mind has been changed through
long apprenticeship. I know the secrets of the ways of being and
becoming. The Moon is attributed to my realm. It is the inner light. See
the Moon at my feet. Moon magic is mine as it is also the magic of all
women who remember the Divine by Her own name. See that my robe
resembles the waters. Moon and water hold the ebb and flow of life
between them. I have access to the living waters within. I know the ways
of the psyche and how it may be nourished. I am your capacity for wisdom
and deep understanding. I bring compassion and gnosis. I am your
realisation of the mystery of life. If you see me in a spread, I affirm your
power to be intuitive and find your own wisdom. I am the High Priestess
in you.

Evocation of the Empress, Tarot Trump III

I am called the Empress. See I am enthroned in my own kingdom which
is the natural world. I raise the sceptre to denote my sovereignty here. I
am bedecked by the crown of stars. Do you think that your world is
separate from the stars above? The Earth and the physical laws which

operate here are but part of a greater reality. I
am here as the Earth Mother of your world. I
am within every birth whether of child or star.
I am the Great Mother, the Empress of the
World. See the corn growing at my feet. I
bring you the gifts of the earth. Has not wheat
sustained you with bread which is the staff of
life? I am the mother of the corn. I show you
the cycle of renewal which is ever present. At
the harvest the corn is reaped, but in the seed
corn there lies your future. When you attend to
my cycles you will flourish. The further we
become estranged, the greater your peril. The
evidence of the five senses may even blind you
to your own predicament, but the five senses

do not perceive the whole. Seek holism and you will find me. I embrace
you and sustain you. Seek holism and you will find the knowing of the
heart. I bring the power of Venus, which is love. See my heart shaped
shield. The circle of spirit surmounts the cross of matter. Spirit and matter
are conjoined in me. Look upon the natural world and see my living forces
flowing in every tree and plant. Embrace my world with open heart and
you will touch the life I offer you. Reach out to me as the Great Mother.
Serve me and I will serve you a thousandfold. Think of me as your mother
and I will welcome you as my children. Abundance can be yours for I still
have much to show to you. Tear me from your hearts and weep for
yourselves. I am your connection with the natural world. I am your ability
to relate to the world of the senses with enjoyment and *joie de vivre*. If you
see me in a spread I remind you of the bounty and abundance of nature. I
ask you to rejoice in the harvest. I am the Empress in you.

Evocation of the Emperor, Tarot Trump IV

I am the Emperor. My consort is the Empress whose bounty is abundant.
I am a ruler of another kingdom. Wherever society and community are to
be found I will arise. Great power is put at my disposal by others who seek
leadership and direction. I meet difficult choices and face weighty
problems constantly. Yet I face these with courage and determination for
I have the best interest of the whole kingdom at heart. My rule reflects
cosmic law. Aries, cardinal fire is assigned to my nature. I am prepared to

utilise the powers of fire which bring creativity and warmth. I am enthroned upon the great stone seat ornamented with ram's heads. I am a natural leader. I inspire confidence in others. I show initiative and I carry a natural authority. I carry the orb and sceptre as symbols of my sovereignty. I bear the energy of Mars which rules Aries. Mars brings me physical courage, robust strength, vitality and dynamism. I am not afraid to defend what calls out for defence and to protect what needs to be protected. I bring order to chaos and regulate the formless with pattern. My power lies in the principles which structure and create, build and transform. My

laws establish parameters. My principles govern possibilities. I am your ability to take control of your own life and make wise and meaningful judgements. I am your power to defend yourself when necessary. I am your power to take a stand on things that matter to you. I am the ruler within. I am your own kingship. I am your ability to lead your life in accordance with the rules you value and follow. I am your ability to govern yourself wisely and well. I accept the responsibilities of running a life for I have all the necessary abilities. If you see me in a spread I bring you decision-making, good choices, sound planning and positive action. I am the Emperor in you.

Evocation of the Hierophant, Tarot Trump V

I am the Hierophant, the revealer of secret things. My title is unfamiliar in this day and age. In another place and time my title was familiar and honoured for I was the High Priest at the Mysteries of Eleusis where the mysteries of being were enacted beneath the veil of secrecy. I am here once more to initiate you into the conscious knowing of your own true being. See that I give blessing which is the blessing of the Mysteries. See the keys at my feet. Through revelation, I can provide you with the key of awakening. See that I wear the garments of the worldly church, yet I am not confined to one time or place. The crown and sceptre are emblems of exoteric religion, which provides the container for the many. Yet the esoteric way is here too enshrined within the outer form. If you would seek the inner within the outer, seek the universal not the particular, seek practice not dogma, seek reality not illusion. Like my brother the Magician, I too am a living bridge. Before me is the domain of the outer world, behind me is the domain of the inner world. I am seated at the threshold where I bring the mysteries of being into the world. I wear the red and the white, the spiritual within the material. My sign is Taurus which is the sign of the Bull and the element of earth. The mysteries which I serve connect heaven and earth. Truth can only be lived in the world. Will you too become the living bridge? I offer you the keys of self-knowledge. Are you ready

to accept them? I am your desire to find a philosophy and to look for meaning in life. I am the teacher within. I am your ability to receive. I am your openness to spiritual teaching. I am the voice of eternal wisdom and timeless truth. If you see me in a spread I ask you to seek wisdom, hear good advice and seek the highest truth you can attain. I am the Hierophant in you.

Evocation of the Lovers, Tarot Trump VI

We are called the Lovers. We are ready to set out on life's path together. Though we are separate, we seek to be one. Though we are apart we seek to be joined. Love brings the desire for unity at all levels of being and expression. The urge to express love is universal and timeless. But who can explain this uniquely intense and powerful human quality? Who does not want to give love and be loved in return? Some call us Adam and Eve. Some call us Shiva and Shakti. Our names do not matter. We have many names. We are the archetypal man and woman, male and female, yin and yang. We each bring our own special qualities to our partnership. As yin

and yang are complementary, we combine to create a balance of opposites. We complement each other. All opposites seek each other constantly for they are part of the same whole. Gemini is assigned to us for we are as twins coming together. Gemini brings the easy mental communication of an air sign, for lovers need to understand each other. We are not alone. Another level of mind is here too. The angelic presence brings the possibility of higher consciousness. Love itself can be the vehicle for a profound awakening to life. The angel blesses both equally with outstretched hands. Yet the superconscious mind is only perceived through the receptive feminine mind. The conscious mind must look towards its partner to be awakened. See the serpent and the Tree of Life – why is the serpent so feared when its symbolism speaks so clearly of renewal and rebirth? We can be renewed through love. We are your willingness to give and receive love. We are your ability to relate, we are your capacity to share and merge, blend and give to another. We affirm your readiness to extend love and be open to its power. In a spread we show you the relationships in your life whether friends or Lovers. We are the lovers within you.

Evocation of the Chariot, Tarot Trump VII

I am known as the Chariot. Here is an unfamiliar vehicle for you. It is a vehicle which requires the most skilful handling and control. The creatures which draw the chariot, whether horses or fabled sphinxes, are wild and independent in their own right. How shall the twin powers be harmonised to serve the chariot and not themselves? See the sphinxes. Here the white and the black are the opposing forces of the dual nature. Yet I have them calmed and tamed. This opposition gives me strength not weakness. See that I stand with confidence in my own chariot. Where are my reins, or my whip? I do not need these to control my chariot. I am master in my own

house. I am the ruler of the kingdom within. I rule from the throne of my own being. See that my chariot is canopied by stars. I too am bedecked by cosmic symbols of star and Moon for I know the cycles of Earth and sky.

I understand my own nature. My house is wherever I am beneath Moon or star. I am free for I work in harmony with the universal laws. See too the green laurel of my brother, the Fool, in my crown. I hold an image of the pristine undivided state. Its memory is always before me as I travel. The sign of Cancer is attributed to me. Cancer is represented by the crab which finds a new home when the old becomes too small. Like the crab, I have dwelled within many different protective shells, each a body for a duration. The Moon rules Cancer, and I wear the lunar crescents at my shoulders like epaulettes. I am the victor in my own kingdom. I am answerable to no one other than my fully realised self. I am your power to take charge of your life. I am your ability to hold the reins of all the competing forces which seek your attention and time. I am your ability to be master in your own house. If you see me in a spread, I show you your own successes and earned victories. I point out your achievement. I am the charioteer within.

Evocation of Strength, Tarot Trump VIII

I am known as Strength. Does my image remind you of another? Do you remember my brother, the Magician? See we are both blessed by the sign of infinity. We are conscious of the infinite life and the cycle of being and becoming. I open the mouth of the lion. I am Strength. See that I am garlanded only with roses. My strength is derived only from the unfoldment of my own spiritual nature. See that I wear only a white robe. My strength lies in the conscious realisation of my own pure being which can never be defeated. I hold the lion in close embrace. My consciousness rules here. I have emerged many times from myself; each birth into new

levels of consciousness has stabilised my inner strength. Leo is attributed to me. He represents the power of fixed fire which is spiritual fire. How often is spiritual presence represented by tongues of flame? The element of fire is the creative spirit itself. As a blade is tempered by fire, so the soul too is finely honed by constant work both inner and outer. Have you been tested by the fires of life? Do you recognise moments of test and challenge as opportunities for the soul's growth? Do you recognise the lion when he seeks you out? He comes in many forms as the opponent, the difficulty and the obstacle. He is the lion barring your way forward. Shall you run and retreat or face his power squarely with your own? The opponent shows you your own strength. Seek out the meaning of spiritual strength and you will be given the means to find it. I am your power to overcome obstacle and difficulties in your life. I am your power to summon reserves in the face of opposition. I am your power to uphold what you believe. I show you that strength comes from within. In a spread I remind you to look within for the source of strength. Draw deeply upon your own reserves. I am Strength within you.

Evocation of the Hermit, Tarot Trump IX

I am the Hermit. I walk alone. I continue on my solitary path without companion or friend. I am led only by my lamp which shows me the path ahead. I am supported by my staff. I am unafraid to journey alone for I have seen every condition and circumstance known by the many. It is all behind me. I have tasted it all. I walk on. See the beacon light which guides me. It is the light of the eternal wisdom. It illuminates the path for others who might seek this path too. All who tread the path make it easier for those who come after. I am indebted to those who trod this way before. All else has been purged from me. My inner sight is sharp. I have known all the ways of men, I have seen

the human heart in all its ways. My words carry prophecy within them. I have walked so long and so far. I am ancient. My journey has been long and I am not finished yet. Virgo is attributed to me, for I am virgin-born of myself. My consciousness has been reborn many times over and shall be again even in these desolate wastes. For my inner life is rich with meaning and understanding. I do not wander aimlessly but with intent. I have left behind all the trappings of the world. I pursue my goal which is to seek myself and in finding myself I shall find the whole which is holy. If you should desire to tread this lonely path too, know that others have trodden the way before you. I have travelled ahead unknown by you, unseen by you. My beacon will shine out as your light will shine out for those who follow. You and I are travellers. I am your ability to bear solitude and to be alone. I am your ability to stand out from the crowd and to walk a different path. I am your ability to be comfortable in your own company. I show you the creative powers of solitude. In a spread I remind you to heed wise advice from an elder or to take a road less travelled. I am the Hermit within you.

Evocation of the Wheel of Fortune, Tarot Trump X

I am called the Wheel of Fortune. I turn within your life as opportunities and possibilities open and close like revolving doors. I am turning all the time. I am never still by night or by day. I am mirrored in the turning of the year and the turning of the ages. I am found in all the cyclic movements both great and small. When you remember my nature, you understand that everything changes. I show you the wheel of becoming. Turn with the wheel. Know that nothing is still. You cannot halt the wheel. Becoming is built into your body as cells are renewed and you are continuously remade. Nothing is still, all is change. See the wheel within the wheel. Here is Rota, the wheel. Here is Tarot. Here is Tora, the law. All is turning. I am

the wheel of fate which binds you to all that has passed before. I am the equilibrating power of karma which is the adjustment of your deeds and the balancing of your pattern. Jupiter is attributed to me. I am the principle of expansion for I am the way of your becoming. See the serpent, here is another symbol of becoming. The serpent renews itself from within. See the four Holy Kerubs. Here are the four elements. Here are the four worlds of archetype, creation, formation and action. At the heart of the wheel lies the mystery of being and becoming. Here are the components of change and the semblance of stability. Here is the paradox of change in stability and stability in change. See the enigmatic Sphinx, the guardian of the wheel, and the bearer of the sword of release. When shall you be released? When shall your becoming be complete? Recognise the wheel. It turns within your life. Salute the wheel. I am your ability to adapt to change and to turn with the wheel. I am your ability to accept the ups and downs of life.

I bring you the certainty that the flow of life cannot be halted. In a spread I show you that change is continuous and not to be feared. I am the Wheel of Fortune in you.

Evocation of Justice, Tarot Trump XI

I am Justice. You already know my nature for when aggrieved you have sought me out. When I am denied, you feel my lack of presence keenly. I am sought everywhere and at all times for I have the power to heal the oldest of wounds. Wherever I am honoured I bring the establishment of law with me. I have done this since the earliest of times. No civilisation reaches maturity without the rule of law. It should be no surprise that Libra is attributed to me for I hold the scales where I balance deeds and intentions, actions and results. I am dressed in two opposing colours for I must balance two opposing claims one against the other. All is weighed, all is balanced. I have been called Maat, the Lady of the Judgement Hall. I am the keeper of the balance in the Hall of Truth. I balance the feather of truth against the actions, deeds and thoughts held by the heart. I am called She Who is Straight for my measure is straight. I am moral truth and uprightness. Even rulers make offerings to me. I am the value you place on truth for without truth no justice can be possible. I am the upholder of truth which is the very heart of law. I am unbiased and without prejudice. The law is impersonal. Justice herself is depicted in contemporary courts of law where she bears the sword and scales. She is often shown blindfolded. I am your karma which adjusts from life. I am your capacity to live by justice in your dealings with friends and family, colleagues and strangers. I am the voice of fair play in your life. I am the voice that speaks for the wronged and the abused. I am the watcher who sees that all is balanced in the scales. I am your ability to understand the viewpoint of another and to comprehend a grievance that is not yours. In a spread I remind you that deep-seated factors may be at work. The present is rooted invisibly in the past. Perhaps a legal solution is indicated too. I am your sense of justice. I am Justice within you.

Evocation of the Hanged Man, Tarot Trump XII

I am the Hanged Man. Does my title disturb you for men are rarely hanged nowadays? Once the hanging tree was a common fate for the criminal. Yet I am no criminal; look into my eyes and you will see a man at peace. In my upside-down world I have a new perspective. I see things differently. For me reality is reversed. I may appear strange, even ridiculous from your perspective. I hang suspended from a living tree which is the Tree of Life. It alone supports me and upholds me and enables me to see everything in a new way. What sustains you in life? Where do you stand? Do you seek fixed values and the certainty of a secure life? Then look in vain,

for what you seek is but illusion. Life is never still. Do I remind you of all the Way-Showers both great and small who chose to hang upon the Tree? To take an upside-down view of life is to become an outsider. As spiritual values begin to turn your life around so you too will find yourself moving away from the values of the many. If you follow the Path, you too will appear to be upside down to those who have not journeyed. So you have a choice. Can you stand on your head and reverse any values which prevent a spiritual view? Are you prepared to live supported by the Tree of Life? Are you prepared to loosen your footing in the world of appearance in order to see what is real? The view from here is universal and timeless. Neptune is assigned to me. It is the planet which symbolises mystical consciousness and loss of self-identity. Who understands the perspective of the mystic except another mystic? I am your willingness to be misunderstood. See I am at peace with myself and the world. I reverse all that you have learned. I offer you a radical new perspective. I am your ability to sacrifice the common goals in search of others. In a spread I show your ability for self-sacrifice. I am your desire to shed what prevents you from a universal vision. I am the Hanged Man within you.

Evocation of Death, Tarot Trump XIII

I am Death. My name has been feared by all who hold life dear. Yet life and death are inseparable realities. I touch all kingdoms, whether animal, vegetable or mineral. I touch everything from the smallest microbe to the mightiest planet. I have a valued place. Imagine only unrestrained growth or indestructible physical life. These would not be gifts but states of regret. I am the balancing principle for I show you the value of what you have. It can be taken away when you least expect it. Live fully through discovery and wonder. Drink deeply of life's cup. Do not ignore my reality. In me all are made equal both the great and the lesser. I am no respecter of earthly power or rank. I meet all in good time. Awareness of my presence will sharpen your taste for life. All spiritual traditions ask you to contemplate my

reality through quiet reflection and contemplation. Face me in this way if you can and I will eventually come to you as a friend. Though it is easy to forget, I walk alongside you in everyday life. Your being is renewed constantly as cells are reborn and remade. You too are reborn and remade as you grow and change. I bring the change that permits life to flow like a great river. I am already present in every cell for life and death flow continuously from pole to pole. See that I, Death carry the banner of resurrection and renewal. See the five petalled rose which symbolises a new birth. See too that the Sun rises on the far banks in my hidden kingdom. The scorpion and the eagle are also mine. These are the dual signs of Scorpio. Here lies my mystery. The one is earthbound, a bringer of death, the other flies high soaring towards the Sun. Deep are my mysteries which you fear to know. Yet I am the bestower of the gift of the eagle, liberation. If you see me in a spread do not fear the worst. I ask you to look at what you are carrying in life. Which burdens may be released so that change can take place? I am your ability to be renewed at all levels of being. I am your ability to release the old and make way for the new. I am your friend. I am Death within you.

Evocation of Temperance, Tarot Trump XIV

I am called Temperance. I am a virtue from the past but perhaps I have something to offer you today. I am not moderation or denial but the tempering of the soul. I stand upon the middle path where I am seen creating a new elixir from the forces presented to me. See that I keep the twin powers in perpetual motion. The waters of life flow from one pole to another without ceasing. When there is stalemate or stagnation I bring release as a skilful negotiator finds the path to resolution. I am also the temperer for as a blade is tempered through fire and water, heat and cold, so I temper your being through circumstances which test your capacity to maintain equilibrium. Every new test is an opportunity to test yourself. I provide the opportunity to put your beliefs into practice and test them against the rigours of people and circumstance. Sagittarius is mine. It brings a

tempering fire to the mind. It is also the arrow of aspiration which propels you forward in life. Sagittarius brings a teaching capacity and I am your ability to learn from the experiences of life. In my angelic form, I represent a voice of higher consciousness. My promptings are heard in the heart. See the yellow iris which stands for Iris, the sister of Mercury. What messages do you hear from your own divinity which is the angel within? Do you hear the voice of temperance which urges counsel and skilful balancing? I am your ability to find equilibrium and tread the middle path. I am your willingness to find a moderate solution and seek compromise. I am your willingness to recognise a testing period and respond with qualities from within. I am your willingness to be tempered by circumstances and people. In a spread I suggest you find a middle way to a problem. I show you that everything you need is to hand. I am the skilful negotiator and the creative resolution. I show how you can skilfully blend opposing factors and facilitate the emergence of a new and creative solution. I am Temperance within you.

Evocation of the Devil, Tarot Trump XV

I am called the Devil. Does my name strike terror into your heart? You laugh and say that you do not believe in me. Here is my first victory then. You discount what lies within and how it may be used to bring you to defeat. I have terrorised generations before you, so why should you be different even in this the age of reason? Does reason free you from fear?

I am all your fears combined and blown up into monstrous proportions. See my horns and goat legs, my bat wings and hideous face. What a devil you have created for yourselves. Are you really fearless, are you truly without fear? When you have no fear you will be free and I will dissolve before your fearlessness. But the truly free soul is a rare event so my kingdom is peopled by the enslaved and the spiritually blind. See my prisoners, how easily they might free themselves or indeed each other. My chains sit loosely upon their necks. I do not bind them to me, they stand here in preference to freedom and light. In truth I am Capricorn. I am earth, I am matter. How do

you regard matter? When you see through the game of materialism you will be free. When you see through the veil of appearance into reality you are free. Until then you will always be afraid that you do not have enough and your fear will lead you to grasp and hold and claim. Status and position are powerful lures for the unwary, possessions and glamour blind you to meaningful interaction. The ladder of material success is steep and hung with fears of your own making. See that these chains are easily removed if you have the will power. I am your self-delusion. I am your greed. I am your desire to possess and own. In a spread I remind you of the folly of materialism and I show you the trap that yawns at your feet. What has enslaved you? What temptations beckon? What price will you pay for reward or recognition? What fear has captured your heart? I am the Devil within you.

Evocation of the Tower, Tarot Trump XVI

I am called the Tower which is no other than the self constructed gradually through life year after year. It rises brick upon brick from your thoughts, desires, intentions and aspirations. What have your life aspirations and hopes built? Have you created a tower of strength for yourself and others? Look carefully upon the tower that you see. Here is the Tower Struck by Lightning, the self electrified by spiritual fire. See the Lightning Flash which lifts the Crown from its base and causes tongues of fire to burn within. Spiritual awakening can take many forms. Waking up can be devastating. The personality is shaken to its very core. Aspirations and intentions change. Desires shift. The tower so carefully built falls. Another will rise in its place constructed from fresh thoughts and different feelings. The edifice of self will rise and fall many times. Yet even as the edifice falls, the foundation still stands. When the personality is finally established in alignment with spiritual forces, the Tower will rise in fullness as a beacon for others. Until then it will be remade many times. I admit the power of alchemical fire which fuses opposites and creates a new amalgam from the old. See the falling bodies of blue and red, fire and water, emotion and mind. These forces shall find a new balance, a better equilibrium in the tower

made new. All is continuously remade and renewed. You too shall be renewed. From your downfall you shall be reconstructed, from your loss will come gain. You shall arise from the ashes like a phoenix. I am your power for renewal. I am your ability to rise again after a fall. I am your ability for reconstruction. I am your sense of self which survives all changes. In a spread I show the upheaval and change which is most often unwanted. Every destruction calls for its own reconstruction. Like the phoenix you can rise from the ashes of your life. I am the Tower within you.

Evocation of the Star, Tarot Trump XVII

I am the Star. Look up into the heavens and you will see my form a million times over. Can you count the stars of the night sky or name them? Here is being beyond your comprehension. Here is a wonderful reality you cannot touch. Here is wonder if you but open your eyes and heart. Here are great wonders of time and space. Look up into the night sky and recall the stories of the stars if you can. Star stories are amongst the oldest tales you have created but they are so quickly forgotten when you no longer look at the stars. Come then, raise your eyes. Seek out the constellations of the zodiac. Star lore is

ancient and universal. Here is a wisdom requiring a different mindset from the mundane and utilitarian. Do you think you are separate from the stars so far above? You too are star born. The sign of Aquarius is attributed to me. I am the Water Bearer to the age appearing in the horizon of your mind. I pour new waters upon the Earth. Perhaps you have felt my presence already. New ideas and belief, new hopes and ideals now spring up where living water touches parched ground. See the star goddess Nut or Nuit, the naked goddess of the heavens. She comes to pour the nourishing waters of mind upon the earth for all that is built or created begins first in the mind. See the seven stars dancing about the central Great Star. Each is a level of your own being. Each is a plane of being. Here is the blueprint of your own nature, sevenfold and radiant. Do you live as a sevenfold being? Are you prepared for the gift that I bring? When will you awaken the stars within? Each age responds to a new cosmic vibration. I am your power for wonder. I am your search for transcendence. I am your delight at the magnitude of infinity. I remind you of the vastness of creation. In a spread I bring you a spiritual blessing, the possibility of new horizons and personal goals of fulfilment. I remind you that your own consciousness has no limits. I am the Star within you.

Evocation of the Moon, Tarot Trump XVIII

I am the Moon. Peoples have looked up towards my changing face and woven my nature into the story of their lives. You have created many stories to explain my different forms and phases. I am reflected in the ancient divinities of the moon. I am seen in Diana, Selene and Hecate who celebrate my three faces. What do you know of my faces, of my cycle of darkness and light? Have you watched me in the night sky or are you oblivious to my kingdom? Have you watched my crescent light appear as if from nowhere? Have you marvelled at the light of my full face? Your ancestors watched me and marked my coming and going with notches and marks.

In this way I have taught the count and the calendar of lights. Though I have no light of my own I have a power of my own. Do I not lift the great waters of your world in daily rhythm? I touch the creatures who swarm in the waters too. For moonlight triggers the instinct to reproduce. Pisces is attributed to me. I share the Piscean nature which is sensitive to the subtle and the invisible. It shares an ability to move with the flow of life and touch the depths of deep soul waters. Do I not send out the call to grow and multiply? My rhythmic light touches plant and creature alike. I oversee the path of biological evolution. See how I watch over the path of life as simple life forms emerge from the pool. Where will this evolutionary path take you, the human species, as you face the next great age? Do not be fooled by the veneer of sophistication which you wear so thinly. You are part of the natural world. You have the power to feel the subtle rhythms of the Earth, Moon and water which are never separate but interconnected. I am your inner light. I am your subjective life of personal response, feeling, intuition, dream and imagination. I am the moonlight in your life. In a spread I remind you to take care under the light of the Moon. Self-deception and illusion are always possible, the psychic realm is a curious landscape. I am the Moon within you.

Evocation of the Sun, Tarot Trump XIX

I am the Sun. I have been present throughout the rise and fall of every civilisation known to the world. I am the radiant heart of your planetary life. I sustain your world with light and warmth. Plants incline to my light and grow green through my energy. Your stately dance around my still centre brings your own seasonal pattern. Your time keeping is derived from our relationship. You have marked the way stations of our cosmic embrace with celebration and ritual. The solstice and equinox points mark your circuit through the heavens. I am Apollo in his chariot and Ra in his solar boat. I am all the solar gods who have crossed the sky in your mythology. I have

inspired the human mind for I am the light bringer. Unlike my sister the Moon who holds sway over the powers of the unconscious, I am sovereign over the powers of conscious awareness. I am the powers to represent and symbolise, abstract, and communicate. I am the ability to plan ahead, remember the past and envisage the passing of time. I bring foresight, insight and hindsight. You are not bound by instinct or trapped in the moment. You are free to weigh choices and evaluate outcomes. You are free to master what is difficult, to learn what is new, to achieve what your forebears could not. You are not limited to concrete reality. You are free to represent your experience through symbols, words, shapes, pictures, even sounds. You are free from the constraint of the moments, the tyranny of the immediate, the limitation of an event. Seek out the bright light of self-consciousness. Seek out your own enlightenment. Will you rejoice beneath the bright light of self-consciousness? I am your power to shine in life. I am your power to light life for others. I am your brilliance and your success. I am your ability to show the way for others. In a spread I bring you vitality and radiance, success and achievement. I show you your own power to solve problems and to master technical and scientific matters. I am the Sun within you.

Evocation of Judgement, Tarot Trump XX

I am called Judgement. My name has been used to hold men in mortal terror. This is not my function for I am the first awakening not the last judgement. See the angelic figure who awakens with a clarion call. Have you heard this summons in your own life? Can you recall the moment of awakening to a deeper reality? It comes in many guises, as crisis or loss, as desperate questing or profound realisation. Many sleep on though the call is sounded continuously in every moment and in every place. What is your choice? Do you wish to drift on in life? Or shall you awaken? Will you drift aimlessly taken by any passing current or shall you arise to the certainty of your true

being? If you choose the path of awakening, self-judgement will arise. You will see your actions, motives and intentions in a new light. Self-awareness will be kindled. You will encounter me as soon as you awaken to the reality of primal fire. There can be no understanding without the exercise of your own judgement. I am your own self-appraisal, your own self-evaluation. Look at yourself through the eyes of a watcher. What do you see? I am the awakening moment of realisation. If you would truly seek to awaken, prepare to burn away the dross accumulated from past actions and forgotten deeds. I bring you the conscious knowledge of your own divine spark, your own living flame. Awaken. I am your power for self-awareness and self-reflection. I am your ability to look at yourself with detached observation. I am your ability to awaken in life. In a spread I show you the value of self-awareness and self-reflection. I remind you of the need for mindfulness in daily life. I am Judgement within you.

Evocation of the World, Tarot Trump XXI

I am called the World, more often now I am called the Universe. As your consciousness expands so your vision of me expands too. I am the universal laws within the universe. What do you understand of the laws behind the world that you see? Do not be deceived by the appearance of solidity and permanence. Do you really believe in appearance? I am never still. All is movement. All is in motion. The dance never ceases and I am the dancer. See my veil which covers my being. If you cannot see beyond the world of appearances, you will be stranded upon the surface of life. You will believe that matter is solid, separate from the sea of unified energy which sustains

it. See my signs, which are the four fixed signs of the Zodiac and the four elements. Here are the Four Holy Kerubs. I dance within the mandala of the living creation for I am Akasa, the fifth element which vivifies all others. I am the spirit of life, the central mystery of being and becoming. I am the subtle within the physical, I am the invisible within the visible. I dance where I dwell and I dwell in everything. I am the hidden dancer, ever moving, never still. I am whole and indivisible. I am the point in the centre where the four and the one are unified. I hold the twin poles of manifestation in my grasp. Duality is the nature of the world. Saturn is attributed to me. Commonly called Father Time, he is the bearer of limitation and restriction. None may oppose the passing of time. Instead, work with me for I hold the secrets of your karmic adjustment in my dance. I offer you opportunities for atonement and recognition. Greet old friends in new guises, hail old enemies as new friends. I am your sense of connection to the greater world. I am your ability to partake in and contribute to the world. In a spread I show you achievement and the completion of a task well done. I am the reflecting mirror in which you dance your life into being. I show you the possibility of travel. I show you a greater vision of what the world has to offer. I show you the vastness of your own being. I am the World within you.

Summary

■ You have experienced the Major Arcana through meditation.

8 CREATING THE TAROT MANDALA: DIVINATION

A layout is a mandala, a circular conceptual framework that mirrors realities and proposes ideals.

James Wanless and Angeles Arrien, *The Wheel of Tarot*

The Tarot Mandala

The word mandala means circle. A circle is perhaps among the oldest and most universal of all symbols. In its form we see the round of the year, the wheel of birth and death and the continuity of life. The circle shows us completion and wholeness. The image of the circle seems to be deeply embedded within us; human life begins as a spherical ovum cell. As divisions of the ovum bring physical complexity, so divisions within the mandala represent the complexity of the psyche. Tibetan Buddhism has developed a rich mandala tradition which operates within a precise code of correspondences. The landscape of the psyche is described in pictorial symbols. When Tarot cards are laid out in a symbolic form we are creating the Tarot mandala, the reflecting mirror of self. Though the mandala requires no validation other than its own long existence, it was Jung who rediscovered the significance of the mandala and made its form intelligible in the West. During 1918–19 he began to draw mandala images. He noted the correspondences between the symbolism and his own inner situation. Jung had merely rediscovered what had never been lost in unbroken spiritual traditions. In his therapeutic work with patients Jung observed the symbols which emerged spontaneously in the healing process. We find an extraordinary accord between such symbols and those represented through the Tarot. We may draw upon the wisdom that Jung rediscovered and apply the same principles to the Tarot. The images of the Tarot may be combined with the form of the mandala to create the Tarot Mandala. Like Jung we may hold the mirror up to the self. In his mandalas Jung saw himself. We too may draw upon the mandala so that we may glimpse the self.

Divination through Tarot is but one means among many. Making patterns to read the greater patterns of our lives is an ancient theme. Casting runes or throwing yarrow stalks: all is about pattern making and reading symbols not words. When we create a Tarot spread we also lay out a pattern. We hope to read the lesser pattern laid out before us as a reflection of a greater pattern that is woven invisibly into the fabric of our lives. Who can doubt the power of human curiosity or the dilemma presented by decision-making? Who has not at some time or other wanted even briefly to steal a momentary glimpse of a future outcome in order to bolster a present decision? Who can blame us, we are after all only human. There is no doubt that it is divination that draws so many people in increasing numbers to Tarot. Divination has its own eternal fascination. How curious it is that we call our attempt to see the bigger picture 'divination', which is clearly derived from the word 'divine'. This relates to something above and beyond human understanding. So through the act of divination do we make a connection to the Divine? If so the act of divination surely assumes a more exalted status than that expressed through telephone Tarot lines or expensive commercial transactions. In fact something decidedly greater than ourselves just might be going on in the meeting of reader and querant, mind and symbol.

It was Jung who put forward the theory of synchronicity which explains not merely the Tarot transaction but a far wider range of phenomena. Synchronicity points to a deep pattern or order which transcends the ordinary space-time framework in which we set ourselves. Coincidences are synchronous events between causes which seem to have no connection. Surely we have all experienced the impact of coincidence which can range from the noteworthy to the extraordinary. The reading is not unlike a managed coincidence in which the chosen cards coincidentally mirror real life. Who can fully explain the dynamics of this interaction? Who has yet found all the answers to the mysteries of mind?

Specific researches into the Tarot are quite unusual but all the more valuable for being rare. Jane English, who is by training a physicist, took the bold step of applying scientific method to the Tarot. Her paper 'A Scientist's Experience with Tarot' opens with an honest and commonly held opinion:

> It is commonly thought that science is incompatible with Tarot, that science is totally logical while Tarot is totally intuitive. For a long time I, too was of this opinion, being committed to a scientific

worldview, would have nothing to do with Tarot. I saw it as a mere fortune-telling device, as something used by the unscrupulous to manipulate and control those who were too lazy to take responsibility for their lives. However, some years after I became as interested in exploring the inner worlds of consciousness as I had been in exploring the outer world scientifically, I met and studied with people who were using Tarot in a way that appealed to me.[1]

The personal conflict between Tarot and science was obvious:

Being both a scientist and a Tarot practitioner I was intensely interested in resolving this conflict.[2]

It was her custom to select three cards daily and record any correlation with her own life experience. She applied statistical analysis to her own two-year record. Additionally, two friends also supplied personal records covering a two-year period. Her own journal provided 1,982 choices, her friends supplied another 2,395 and 2,015 selections respectively. It has to be stated that the personal journals were prepared long before the idea of statistical analysis was suggested. She used a control pack of 78 index cards blank on one side and numbered on the other. These were shuffled like the Tarot cards but chosen without any meditative preparation. Additionally a computer was programmed to perform the same process: 13 runs were made totalling 24,183 selections. Of the 13 runs, nine produced a probability of non-randomness of less than 50 per cent; two runs produced a probability of 53 per cent and only one run reached a statistical probability of 65 per cent. The probability of non-randomness for the selections made by the three individuals stood at 95 per cent for each of the journals. The probability of non-randomness using the index cards stood at 53 per cent. The results were indeed thought-provoking as Jane English recognised:

Saying the choice is random is the same as saying that the cards are totally separate from the person who picks them. Saying that the choice is not random is to say that there is a connection between the persona and the cards. After doing all the analysis I was struck with the reality of the connectedness of the cards and the person who chooses them in meditation even though my old scientific belief system asserted that there was no connection. The statistical analysis doesn't show the nature of the connection between the person and the cards; it just shows that it is very probable that there is a connection of some kind.[3]

Parapsychological studies have long shown us that emotional unconscious factors play a significant role in lowering the inhibitory mental threshold. If we look at the traditional ambience surrounding a Tarot reading, we find a number of procedures which shift awareness into an open receptive mode. Shuffling the cards, a moment of meditation, attunement for guidance, even an expectant silence shifts us away from ordinary thinking. It is significant that Tarot cards are never laid out in the matter of fact manner Jane English dealt out the numbered index cards. What might we expect if this were the case? Let us now look at the process of divination in more detail.

Preparation for divination

Therefore the diviner should enter upon divination with a mind clear and unprejudiced, neither disturbed by anger, fear, nor love, and with a sound knowledge of the correspondences of the symbols.

Robert Wang, *The Golden Dawn Tarot*

Laying out a spread can be as simple or as ornate a process as you wish it to be. Robert Wang, following in the tradition of the Golden Dawn, suggests an elaborate procedure.

Also it may be well for the diviner to put on his insignia, and make over the pack any invoking hexagram or pentagram, either with the hand alone, or with convenient magical instruments. He continues, 'In the divine name IAO, I invoke Thee thou Great Angel HRU who art set over the operation of this Secret Wisdom. Lay thine hand invisibly on these consecrated cards of art, that thereby I may obtain true knowledge of hidden things to the glory of the ineffable Name. Amen.'[4]

Such a specialised preparation is, of course, only relevant to practitioners of this tradition but its essential purpose is clear. The affirmation attunes the reader to the task in hand and serves to open a channel into the unconscious and emotional realm. The same thing can be accomplished in many ways. It is best if you devise your own method of attunement. It should include a gentle withdrawal into your own inner space and an opening to spiritual guidance in a chosen form. Having found an approach that you like, use it every time as your own opening. Divination, laying out a spread, follows a regular pattern which also serves to link the operator into the realm of Tarot. The stages are as follows:

1 Choosing a significator

Choose a court card to represent the querant.

2 The question

Ask the querant to frame the question clearly. The question may be kept private or disclosed. It should cover only one topic. Vague questions will elicit vague answers.

3 The shuffle

The significator is laid out. The seeker is given the deck to shuffle and is asked to think about the question while shuffling. When the pack is shuffled the querant is asked to cut the pack most often into three piles face down. Next the pack is recombined by the questioner. If the reader is sitting beside the querant, the cards are already facing the right way. If the reader is seated opposite to the querant, the pack will need to be turned to face the reader. Open the cards like a book from left to right.

4 The spread

Know which spread you are going to use beforehand. Select a spread which reflects your own experience and the needs of the client. Don't use a complicated or lengthy spread for a new client until you are familiar with its dynamics. On the other hand, don't be afraid to try a new spread. Don't get stuck in the rut of only being able to read from one spread. Read often for friends and family and for yourself too. Be prepared to learn from this practice. Make notes and see how cards and life circumstances correlate. Build up your own vocabulary of correspondences. There is something to be learned from every reading and every interaction.

5 The interpretation – learning to read patterns

This is the art of blending all that you understand into a meaningful synthesis. There is a place here for both the intellect and the intuition. Use the intellect to analyse the structure of the reading. Use the intuition to weigh and evaluate the correspondences expressed within the symbolic pictures. Intellectually assess the following:

- What is the strongest suit?
- What is the second most dominant suit?
- Which suit is absent?
- Are there any reversed cards?

■ What is the balance of court cards to the whole?
■ What is the balance of Minor Arcana cards to the whole?
■ What is the balance of Major Arcana cards to the whole?

This basic analysis will draw the threads of the reading together and lay the foundation for the work of the intuition. This function is only strengthened through practice, so let's practise.

Tarot spreads: symbolic patterns

The Tarot encourages you to look at life symbolically.

Mary Greer, *The Wheel of Tarot*

Although some spreads remain popular, there is no reason why you cannot devise your own spread. The spread needs to include meaningful categories if it is to make sense. A spread represents a meaningful human pattern. A Tarot spread is a symbolic pattern. So let us begin with the simplest symbolic representation and move gradually towards more complex patterns. It is common to choose a significator card to represent the querant, the questioner. So we will begin with this simple correspondence: choose a significator to represent yourself.

Be able to explain your choice. Have you represented a deep quality in yourself or have you chosen to represent the type of problem that occupies you currently? Will your significator be the same next week or tomorrow? Now we will begin to build on this basic representation. Today, yesterday and tomorrow are linked in a continuous cycle of change so let's use the Tarot to represent past, present and future. Before laying down your cards decide how best you wish to symbolise these three categories. There are many possibilities. Be experimental before you finally settle on a symbolic pattern that is meaningful to you. We will begin with a very simple pattern which recognises the factor of time in human life. We will begin with the simplest of divisions into past, present and future.

Linear spreads

As time appears to be linear to us, you might simply lay out three cards in a row. In this sequence it would seem natural to place the significator at

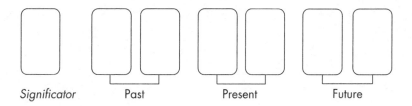

Significator   Past   Present   Future

Figure 8.1   Past, present, future

the start. Do you think that one card is sufficient to represent each category? You might like to lay two cards in each place (see Figure 8.1).

This is clearly a very general categorisation which can be broken down further. The past has many connotations from a recent event to deep-seated attitudes or even far memory. The present too poses many questions for us. The open-ended future contains many possibilities as it is the place where we project hopes, wishes, aspirations and intentions. Additionally the short-term and long-term future are clearly quite different. So it is clear that we can begin to subdivide these three basic categories:

- What further questions might clarify issues from the past?
- What further questions might clarify issues in the present?
- What further questions might clarify issues concerning the future?

We do so much weekly planning that we are deeply conditioned to think in seven-day spans. Try a simple seven-card reading and see how this relates to the events of the forthcoming week (see Figure 8.2). Observe the events of your week with detachment and make notes on any correspondences that seem significant. Expand on the idea of representing the week and turn it into a month. To keep things simple, let one card represent the major focus of each week (see Figure 8.3).

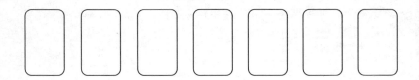

Figure 8.2   The week ahead

Figure 8.3   The month ahead

Circular spreads

The concept of time seems to be intimately related to all methods of divination and Tarot is no exception. Becoming aware of how past, present and future are interrelated in your own life will make you more sensitive to the flow of events represented in any given spread. So take a Tarot card on a daily basis and see how it relates to the events of your life. Keep a record of your choices and note any correspondences that appear. The present soon becomes the past and the future soon becomes the present. This personal record keeping is good practice. Though time appears to be linear, at a deeper level it is also seasonal and cyclical so you may find a circular spread more satisfying. Some spreads lend themselves especially well to the passing of time. The 12 months of the year naturally suggest a 12-card arrangement (see Figure 8.4). The 12 cards can also be read in conjunction with astrological correspondences. The 12 cards take on the astrological significance of the 12 houses of the zodiac which in total presents an encompassing view of the individual. Each of the 12 cards may also be read in relation to the time-frame represented by the astrological sign. If you don't feel confident about astrology take 12 cards to represent the 12 months ahead in a straightforward way.

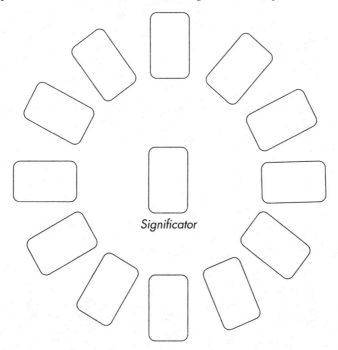

Significator

Figure 8.4   The circle of time

It always seems natural to place the significator at the centre of any circular spread. If you are going to lay around a central card, you need to decide where you will place the card representing the past, present and future. To me it feels natural to represent the past to the left of the significator, the future to the right and the present above the significator.

If you are in sympathy with this arrangement, you have already begun to construct the popular Celtic Cross spread.

The Celtic Cross

No one seems to know how this spread began. However, the standing Cross is common throughout Ireland, a country where spiritual and psychic currents run deep. Unusually, although such crosses are carved with Biblical scenes, the standing cross incorporates a circle and is often decorated with spiral interlocking designs which are symbols of a pagan current. Perhaps it was these ancient monuments which inspired the Celtic Cross spread. The layout contains all the elements of the cross (see Figure 8.5). The upright is displaced to the right while both the circle and cross are represented by the same six cards. There is some variation in the way the spread is read so you will have to find the way you prefer. Mary Greer describes the first six cards as the four cardinal points and the two directions, above and below, which are also the sky/father and the earth/mother. The cards placed in the vertical to the right represent the way, path or ladder on which one travels in life.

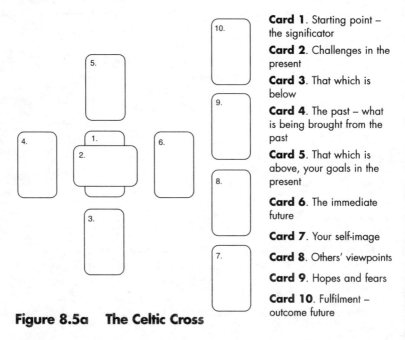

Card 1. Starting point – the significator

Card 2. Challenges in the present

Card 3. That which is below

Card 4. The past – what is being brought from the past

Card 5. That which is above, your goals in the present

Card 6. The immediate future

Card 7. Your self-image

Card 8. Others' viewpoints

Card 9. Hopes and fears

Card 10. Fulfilment – outcome future

Figure 8.5a   The Celtic Cross

Figure 8.5b   A Celtic Cross

You might also like to experiment with the following symbolic form, the Key of Life or ankh. It is not unlike the Celtic Cross – it also contains a circle, a cross and an upright (see Figure 8.6).

- Where will you lay your first card?
- How many categories will you have?
- What will your categories represent?

Figure 8.6   The Key of Life – use this basis to create your own spread

Other symbolic spreads

Time is certainly a useful basis for building a spread. But it is clearly not the only way of categorising ourselves. We might instead look more at constructing a personal profile (see Figure 8.7). A circular spread seems compatible with the idea of looking at the whole life. A circle divides naturally into four, eight or twelve parts. Four sections would seem a little brief, twelve might seem a little ambitious, but eight sections provide enough scope to get an overall impression. Make your own choice of categories before you start. Lay your chosen significator at the centre. You can choose either a number of separate categories or perhaps select four main areas, such as career, health, relationships, money, and elaborate on these through either two or three sections. This would provide the possibility of looking at either present/future, or past/present or even past/present/future, depending on whether you use two or three sections for each heading. The main point to stress is that you do not have to stick to one spread or even one commonly used spread. Be bold and experiment with layouts.

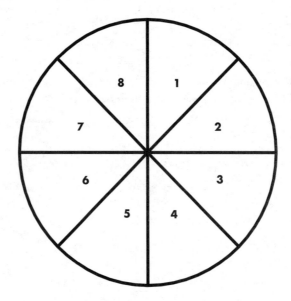

Figure 8.7   A personal profile

Deeply etched patterns and symbols also make firm foundations for Tarot spreads. The mind/body/spirit triangle is now commonly understood. This was the simple theme that Jane English used in her own work over a two-year period with good effect. This is a simple but potentially powerful layout (see Figure 8.8). The same idea can be represented with different formats, either as a linear sequence or as a triangle.

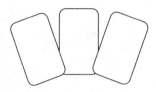

Figure 8.8   Mind, body, spirit

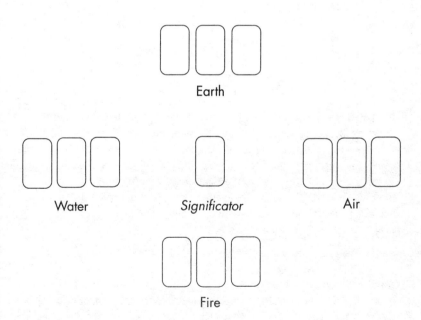

Earth

Water   *Significator*   Air

Fire

Figure 8.9   The element spread

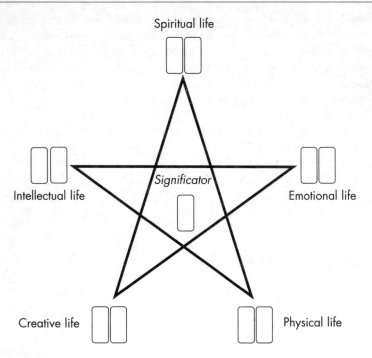

Figure 8.10   The pentagram spread

As the Tarot itself incorporates the elements, we have a ready-made structure which we can use in more than one way (see Figure 8.9). Decide whether you wish to use the four elements as your basis or to include the fifth which brings in the specific possibility of looking at spiritual issues. Place the significator card at the centre and then lay out four groups of three cards to represent earth, air, fire and water. Interpret each group in accordance with the basic elemental attributions already described.

If you prefer to incorporate the element of Akasa in your reading, you might like to try the pentagram spread which is built around the image of the five-pointed star (see Figure 8.10). This structure works well especially if the pentagram is a personal sacred symbol. Another symbol which can be used as a basis for a Tarot spread is the Tree of Life, which provides an in-depth reading (see Figure 8.11). This is quite a specialised structure but if you are working with a Qabalistic approach to Tarot, it provides a good opportunity to develop your understanding of Qabalistic principles.

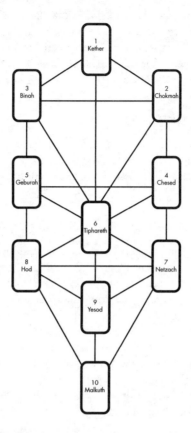

1 Relationship to Spiritual Source
2 Relationship to Great Father, archetypal yang energy
3 Relationship to Great Mother, archetypal yin energy
4 Relationship to forces of outgoing deconstruction
5 Relationship to forces of incoming reconstruction
6 Relationship with higher consciousness
7 Relationship with emotional and creative mind
8 Relationship with intellectual reasoning mind
9 Relationship with personal unconscious
10 Relationship to material world

Figure 8.11   The Tree of Life

We began with the idea of a spread as a mandala, so let us close with a spread specifically laid out as mandala (see Figure 8.12). It presents us with three levels of explanation. You can, of course, create your own mandala spread. The authentic mandala tradition is deep and ancient. The mandala has much to teach us.

Reading patterns

I found that Tarot helped me to focus intuition and perception and to find within myself a deep and true kind of knowing. It helped me to perceive aspects of myself of which I am ordinarily not aware. I used it as a tool for clarifying and getting new perspectives on situations in my life.

Jane English, *The Wheel of Tarot*

The art of divination is all about reading patterns. If the symbols represented by the cards have been sufficiently internalised and inwardly vitalised, the relevant meaning speaks for itself. Intellectual information turns into intuitive synthesis and flows into wise counsel. If you have not already discovered this for yourself, hopefully that moment will arise in the future. Although it is very tempting, try not to become too reliant on lists of meanings. Look at the cards directly in relation to their placement and relation to one another. Move into your own meditative calm and let the still small voice of the intuition speak for you. As you become familiar with the language of the Tarot you will get used to reading its patterns. Look out for the following shorthand:

- **Beginnings**: the Wheel of Fortune, the Fool, the Star.
- **Endings**: the Tower, Death, the Wheel of Fortune, the World.
- **Love and romance**: the Lovers, Ace of Cups, Two of Cups.
- **Partings**: Eight of Cups, Three of Swords, Five of Swords, Two of Discs.
- **Heartache, disappointment**: Ten of Swords, Five of Cups, Three of Swords.
- **Money**: Ace of Discs, Four of Discs, Ten of Discs, Page of Discs.
- **Legal matters**: Seven of Swords, Justice, Judgement.
- **Victory, achievement**: the Chariot, the Sun, Six of Wands.

THE MANDALA OF BEING

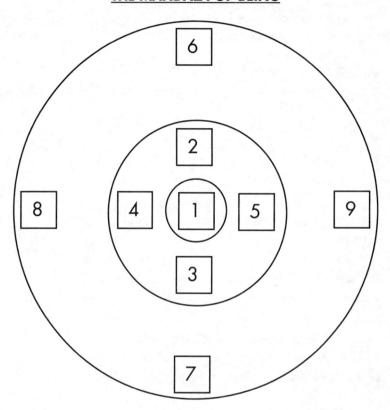

1 Spiritual connection
2 Head: awareness through the mind
3 Heart: awareness through feelings
4 Feminine expression
5 Masculine expression
6 Interaction with resources and finances
7 Interaction with others
8 Life at home
9 Life at work

Figure 8.12 The mandala of being

- **Travel**: the Knights, Eight of Wands, Six of Swords, the Chariot.
- **Spiritual interests**: the High Priestess, the Hermit, the Moon, the Hierophant.
- **New enterprises**: the Magician, the Fool, the Ace of Swords.
- **Working partnerships**: Two of any suit, the Lovers.
- **Creativity**: Page of Cups, Ace of Cups, Ace of Wands, Seven of Wands.
- **Sacrifice**: the Hanged Man.

And here is a quick guide to the Major Arcana:

Trump 0: a beginning, originality, spirituality, folly and eccentricity in material matters.

Trump I: constructive power, initiative, skill, activity, cleverness.

Trump II: wisdom, fluctuation, secrecy, things hidden, deep issues, intuition.

Trump III: fertility, fruitfulness, abundance, happiness, maternity.

Trump IV: stability, power, reason, control, authority, ambition.

Trump V: revelation, the influence of organised religion, spiritual teachings.

Trump VI: love, partnership, personal relationships, marriage, inspiration.

Trump VII: triumph, victory, success, self-assertion, travel.

Trump VIII: courage, spiritual strength, self-mastery, fortitude.

Trump IX: wisdom, the lone pioneer, prudence, inner counsel, divine inspiration.

Trump X: the cycles of life, an unexpected turn, a change.

Trump XI: legal affairs, justice, a judgement, decision.

Trump XII: surrender, an act of sacrifice, unconventional behaviour.

Trump XIII: the end of a phase, a new beginning, transformation.

Trump XIV: balance, partnership, good prospects.

Trump XV: bondage, material desires, a trial, obsessions.

Trump XVI: failure, the crash of expectations, re-evaluation, unfulfilled ambition.

Trump XVII: a blessing, hope, insight, a gift, a promise.

Trump XVIII: organic change, hidden currents, uncertainty, dissatisfaction.

Trump XIX: enlightenment, joy, success, prosperity.

Trump XX: decision, change of direction, final settlement, waking up.

Trump XXI: completion of a cycle, success, achievement.

Summary

- ■ You have been introduced to the principles of divination.
- ■ You have been introduced to a number of spreads.
- ■ You are invited to explore and experiment and to gaze upon the reflections of life in the Tarot mandala.

9 LIVING THE TAROT: THE INVITATION TO LIFE

The secrets of the Tarot are to be found in the Tarot itself. There is no need for an instructor other than itself. It is in itself a book of universal wisdom, its images are not closed secrets demanding elucidation by another, but are a personal invitation to the dance, the great dance of the heavenly fool.

Gareth Knight, *The Treasure House of Images*

The turning point

There can be no doubt that many people have encountered gratifying and lasting personal life change through the Tarot. This may seem to be a high sounding, perhaps even an absurd claim for the effect of what amounts to no more than a series of pictures. Yet it remains incontestably true. So long as we see Tarot as only a series of pictures, our view of its possibilities and potential remains inadequate. Only when we have passed through the Tarot picture into the realm of living archetypes, can we begin to appreciate the value, versatility and creative potential of the image. The moment we accept that Tarot can hold a deeper personal significance, we are free to move beyond a one-dimensional expectation and explore who we are through its reflecting lens. In 1978 Tarot was offered as a credited course at the California Institute of Integral Studies in San Francisco. Such validation is an important landmark in the development of Tarot. This acceptance placed Tarot in a new and contemporary arena where psychologists and therapists could explore its uses. Tarot itself has journeyed from the exoteric game to the esoteric system and has now become a therapeutic tool. The Mystery Schools and the therapeutic process have something in common. Both hold up the mirror of self to the individual. It is perhaps not so surprising that Tarot has moved from one domain to another; much territory is shared. Self-knowledge is at the heart of both the therapeutic and spiritual encounter.

As we explore the new directions in which Tarot is now moving, we may indeed be surprised. At its leading edge Tarot has moved far beyond mere fortune telling. The introductory comments in the book *New Thoughts on Tarot* bring us up to date.

> The primary development in contemporary Tarot has been in readings, we have come a long way from the simple formulas once found in popular instruction books. The Newcastle Symposium, shows how useful a tool a reading has become, not only for self knowledge, but for transformation, for when we know ourselves, and why we do the things we do, we can begin the process of deliberate change, using the Tarot images to help us move into new ways of being.[1]

Let us now explore this new interface.

The invitation to become yourself

> Individuation is the goal of life and the way one becomes truly one's self – the person one was always intended to be.

Demarris S. Wehr, Jung and Feminism

It was Jung who introduced the term 'individuation'. He used it to refer to the process by which a person becomes a psychological individual, whole and complete in themselves. Do we ever stop to consider that most often we are less than we might be? When the reality of this realisation dawns, we are driven on relentlessly towards self-realisation. The gap between the actual and the potential is very often a chasm. Actual behaviour can be the accumulated response not of authentic choice but of early conditioning and other people's expectations. The immature personality clings to second-hand values and strives to please everyone else. The source of personal creativity and inspiration is never found; life is lived only at the surface. Social and material rewards never compensate for the loss of personal meaning. When life only offers materialistic goals and places little value on personal development, our need for avenues of growth and the company of souls becomes more heartfelt. When religion has been stripped of the numinous and become a matter of morality and observance, we sense a vacuum which we cannot name. When technology becomes master and not servant, we are in danger of never finding ourselves. Recognising and distinguishing the many factors and forces which run like invisible computer programs enables us to find out who we really are. Self-knowledge is a long journey.

In the Western Mysteries the journey towards self-knowledge begins with the injunction 'Know Thyself'. This is the starting point. We so often have to struggle to find this first realisation. Only then does the journey to find authenticity really begin. Assagioli commends us to the journey of becoming:

> Spiritual development is a long and arduous journey, an adventure through strange lands full of surprises, difficulties and even dangers. It involves drastic transmutation of the 'normal' elements of the personality, an awakening of potentialities hitherto dormant, a rising of consciousness to new realms and a functioning along a new inner dimension.[2]

We have already related Assagioli's symbols of transcendence with the symbols of the Tarot, we can again apply his words to in-depth interaction with the Tarot. Psychosynthesis offers us four stages of accomplishment:

1 A thorough knowledge of one's personality.
2 The control of its various elements.
3 The realisation of one's true self – the discovery of a unifying centre.
4 The formation or reconstruction of the personality around a unifying centre.

These four stages make up the path of Psychosynthesis. The Tree of Life offers its 22 stages or paths but both schemas have much in common. In these maps of becoming, the journey is facilitated by symbol. We have already noted how the four elements appear in both the Tarot and the Tree of Life. These four ways serve to initiate the first work on the personality. These elemental symbols can be used as an introduction to self-knowledge with powerful effect. The therapist Charloe Wittine employs a sequence of visualisation exercises to establish a sense of reconnection to the energies represented by the elements. She also uses an exercise which she calls 'The Magician's Garden'. It is significant that it serves in exactly the same capacity as the exercise 'The Table of the Elements'. Her clients first approach the Magician as holder of the four elements, through an inner journey. This experience is deepened when the same encounter is translated into a ritualised activity.

> Placed on a table are representations of a wand, cup, sword and pentacle. My client or group and I stand around the table. After centering and a relaxation exercise, I begin by picking up one of

the elements from the table. As I hold it, I begin to get in touch with the feeling and symbolism of the object, as I do, start to express myself verbally and in body position *as* this element. For instance 'I am the cup. I am a vessel of receptive plasticity. I flow and change, moving with the tides, my nature contains the reflections of the universe in its very depths.' When I have finished, the object is passed onto the client who spontaneously impersonates this element. The client has the opportunity to get in touch experientially with these four basic elements.[3]

Such seemingly simple encounters can serve as major turning points in life. The Tarot has many more experiences to offer the individual on the path to individuation.

The invitation to transformation

> The Tarot deck, when used as a symbolic language of transformation, can greatly facilitate connection with and evocation of higher states of consciousness.
>
> Karen Turner, *Transformational Beliefs and Tarot*

We so often speak of transformation and Tarot in the same breath that we can benefit by exploring the concept a little more deeply. Transformation implies a change from one state of being to another, from one identification to another. Above all else it implies movement. It is the antithesis of the static, the inflexible and the rigid. Yet how often do the circumstances of life conspire to push us into a single mould and wear only a single identity? As soon as we become truly identified with but one label, we preclude all others. When we define ourselves with the false certainty of precision, we cast identity into stone which can never bend but only break. The Tarot offers us many identities, each powerful in its own way. As we take on the transpersonal garments of a greater identity, we can step beyond the limits of the personality with all its programming and conditioning. As the four elements of the Minor Arcana take us into working with the personality, so the cards of the Major Arcana take us into the work of reconstructing the personality around a new centre. The Tarot offers us 22 living spiritual garments to try for size. We should be able to try them on one by one. Ask yourself now, which role are you currently wearing, student, homemaker, businessperson, wife, mother, partner, father, lover? Briefly sense your own change of identity as you exchange these everyday garments for those of the Wise Hermit, the Skilful Magician, the Far-Seeing Priestess or Spiritual Strength. Feel how these greater identities expand and empower the roles you already occupy.

We can begin to appreciate the deeper realms of Tarot through testament and case history. The Jungian counsellor Anne Stine, speaks from her personal experience:

> As a result of working with Tarot symbolism in my own life and in consultation with individuals, couples and groups, I found myself noticing that something very significant and powerful occurred, namely, specifically heightened sensitivity to one's internal life and external life; a willingness to see this life differently; an increased participation in choices and decision-making, and a stronger health profile – mentally, emotionally and psychologically.[4]

These positive and life affirming changes are surely those that we all value and seek. Yet so often these are the very qualities that elude us in life as we struggle to balance the competing demands of home and work, career and family, head and heart. Transformation is not an overnight event but a gentle and organic movement from one state of awareness to another. Charloe Wittine recommends a period of between six and nine months' daily visualisation with a chosen image. This may seem unduly long. The time frame really depends upon a number of factors. Ease and familiarity with the interior self through meditation and awareness makes the process of internalisation far quicker. The gestation period, whether it consists of weeks or months, always serves to plant the seed deeply in the unconscious mind and permits a creative transformation to emerge. We have already offered a technique which opens the door to dialogue and guidance with the archetypal energies of the Tarot. This approach may be taken a step further as we move from seeking guidance to seeking a shift of identity. Do not expect this formula to serve you unless you have already established an inner connection through the fundamental exercises. This approach should grow naturally from your own exploration to the archetypal figures.

IDENTIFYING WITH ARCHETYPAL FIGURES

1 Select the Tarot Trump/archetype/character that you wish to work with.

2 Hold the card in the mind's eye. Visualise all its details.

3 Use the card as a doorway. Enter the scene and take the place and pose of the character depicted. Feel that you are now looking outwards through the doorway back into the world of your ordinary life.

4 Become fully aware of what you experience as you take on this greater identity.

5 When you are ready to close, pass back through the doorway. See that the Tarot character occupies the office of the card once more. Allow the scene to fade and fully dissolve all images.

6 Record your experiences.

The following testament briefly indicates the insight that can be gained from such an encounter.

I enter the landscape of Tarot Trump VII, The Chariot. I see the Charioteer. I feel myself walking towards him. I step up into the chariot. I am unsure whether he will step down as I get in. Instead I feel myself merging into his archetypal form. I become aware of changes in my body. My legs become muscular and strong. I have a great sense of connection to the earth through them. I am aware that my body seems to expand and take on tone and strength. My shoulders broaden. My hands increase in size. I feel charged in this form and ready to accept any challenge. I feel the strength of the breastplate around my chest. My head is crowned with a star. I sense a connection with the infinite and the eternal through it. I sense the movement of the chariot. We are moving through my life. I look forward and I see the two sphinxes propelling me onwards. I see the back of their heads and their powerful bodies. At this moment I know I can control them both equally. I mentally give the command to cease, and absolutely and at once the chariot is utterly still. The two sphinxes await my thoughts. Their backs ripple with power but neither will move without my word. Here are the opposing forces and competing demands of my life. Inwardly I see what these represent. The people, places, circumstances, commitments and intentions of my waking ordinary life arise in my mind. I see them all. I sense my power and vigour in life and I understand beyond a shadow of doubt that I am in control of the life that is mine.

I know that my work here is now complete. I feel my consciousness disengage. I see myself walk back through the doorway into the world of everyday experience. I spend a few more moments in quiet contemplation of the Chariot then I reduce the Tarot Trump to a card size and dissolve all the images I have created.

This inner encounter has the power to transform interaction in outer life. It affirms the sense of personal control through deep identification. Every encounter has the power to release inner energies and mobilise existing personal qualities. You are free to encounter any of the Tarot energies at a level of engagement which meets your needs. You will surely be changed by the process.

The invitation to ceremony

Ritual is undoubtedly a powerful technique, as is all group work that involves the controlled use of the creative imagination.

Gareth Knight, *The Treasure House of Images*

Meditation is most often a silent and solitary activity, but it can also be extended into a shared group experience. This changes the dynamics greatly. Minds working as one and in harmony have a power and intensity all of their own. Group work asks for co-operation, co-ordination and to an extent simple orchestration, so that all participants are attuned to the proceedings at all times. The application of this formula takes us from meditation to meditative ceremony. As we have already noted the Order of the Golden Dawn incorporated the sequence of Tarot experiences into its graded work through the Tree of Life. Tarot and transformative ceremony have a long history.

A ceremonial setting for meditation provides a structure which enhances creativity and inspiration by deepening personal response and focusing awareness. A ceremonial form requires a formalised beginning and ending which clearly mark the boundaries of the event. This can range from a simple statement to an elaborate opening, invocation and dedication. The length or complexity need only serve the purpose of the event. A simple and clear opening is quite sufficient: 'We are met to reflect upon the significance and meaning of the Roots of the Powers of the Elements.' The opening should be followed by a brief period when all participants centre themselves inwardly. Ceremony provides the opportunity to utilise and present the relevant symbols in actuality. As Charloe Wittine has indicated the contact with physical symbols can be a powerful moment for change. A meditation on the Empress might be deepened if all participants bring gifts from the earth such as flowers, fruits, seeds, stones, etc. A meditation on the High Priestess might be accompanied by a scrying bowl or mirror. A group meditation on the Star might be deepened by including wonderful starry images of distant galaxies and nebula. The purpose of such ceremonial presentation is always to deepen the personal understanding of the archetype at the centre of the event. Time should be permitted for meditation and personal inner response. A guided visualisation might form the central pivot of the event. Theatricality should never obscure intent. Complexity for its own sake has little value. So keep proceedings simple and clear. This kind of deep inner exploration will have its impact upon all participants, so any group embarking on this voyage of discovery needs to set out in the spirit of mutual support and trust. As the group develops and coheres, longer and more complex Tarot rituals become possible. Short sequences of Tarot Trump can be used in one extended meditation and ultimately it is possible to include the whole cycle of 22 Trumps in one event. Long ceremonial presentations require a high level of concentration. So don't run before you can walk in such matters. The Tarot offers endless permutations and possibilities, it just awaits your creative vision.

The invitation to journey

Tarot is the story of life. It has been my whole life.

Eileen Connolly, *Pathways to Understand the Major Arcana*

The creativity of the Tarot clearly lends itself to structured study and extensive interaction. When combined with the dynamics represented by the Tree of Life, the invitation to journey becomes an invitation to undertake a course of personal development and self-realisation. In the tradition of the Golden Dawn, The Builders of the Adytum currently offer a lengthy training based on the Tarot and Tree of Life in combination. An overview of the training shows us how Tarot images provide significant keys to the journey of becoming. The courses cover a seven-year period of commitment.

- Introduction to the Tarot: 11 weeks, names, numbers, Hebrew letters and basic symbolism of the Tarot keys.
- Tarot fundamentals: 47 weeks, students colour their own keys as an act of meditation.
- Tarot interpretation: 32 weeks, studying the keys in relation to one another.
- The master pattern: 18 months, the Tree of Life and the Tarot.
- Sound and colour: the vibratory power of words and numbers.
- The great work: 12-stage course based around the signs of the zodiac in combination with the Tarot keys.
- Esoteric extension of Tarot to develop supersensory powers: 12 months, entering the Tarot landscapes to set the symbols in motion.
- Esoteric astrology: 52 weeks, astrological symbolism relating to the Tarot keys, connections with chakras.
- Qabalistic doctrines on sexual polarity: transmutation of sexual energy to cosmic wholeness through meditations on relevant Tarot keys.

Clearly such a course demands a high level of commitment to the journey of becoming. It is not untypical of the curriculum offered by contemporary Mystery Schools. The student is gradually brought into a deeper and deeper relationship with both the Tarot and the Tree of Life. These twin symbol systems take the individual beyond personal psychosynthesis into the realms of transpersonal psychosynthesis where the journey into self takes on a deeper and greater significance.

The journey does not have to be structured as a course of study – it can also be free and meandering like a leading thread in the labyrinth of life. The Tarot will lead of its own accord as it has done for both Eileen Connolly and Mary Greer whose lives have unfolded around and through the Tarot. You can journey with the Tarot as a guide and teacher, a constant companion or an occasional friend. You have the power to make these choices.

The invitation to creativity

> I studied English literature and theatre arts and in 1967 discovered the Tarot somehow realising that it would become the basis of my life's work.
>
> Mary Greer, *Women of the Golden Dawn*

There is no doubt that the continuing emergence of new Tarot packs is itself a testament to the enduring and creative power of Tarot. Its language fires the human imagination time after time. It is a well-spring that never runs dry. Human creativity takes infinite forms: pictures, images, representations, models, poems, interpretations, stories, songs, dances, plans, ideas and visions. Tarot offers creativity to anyone willing to be engaged by it. The Tarot is so often used in relation to personal crisis that it is valuable to see it as a source of artistic creation. We are so fast to abandon our own creative impulses. We see creativity reflected in others, in the famous and the established, in the historical and in the applauded, in the modern and in the celebrated, but so rarely do we see creativity in ourselves. Tarot imagery seems unique in its capacity to enter the subconscious mind and reappear in dream images.

Creative dreaming is the prerogative of no single person or group. It belongs to everyone and it is often through the dream that new ideas incubate. Interacting deeply with the symbols of the Tarot enriches the symbolic vocabulary of the mind. This is a wonderfully expansive and creative process which can be used to inspire any number of ventures. Tarot images have been painted, sculpted, drawn, rendered in ceramic and photograph, embroidered, explored as poetry, prose and psychodrama; the possibilities remain endless. The writer Judith Bolinger speaks of her own experience:

> Late in 1973, I began to keep a dream journal. Out of these experiences poems began to emerge, and I began to realise that my writing had a life of its own, that my dream/fantasy experiences moved through me and surfaced as words almost on their own. I was compelled to write, and found it sometimes emotionally painful and sometimes a joyfully light experience, but always with a sense of nourishment once I had expressed myself on the page.

She began to intensify her own dream and fantasy life with images from
the Tarot. Using guided imagery, she entered the Tarot landscape and
began to engage with the characters of the Major Arcana as inner drama:

> The Tarot essentially became for me a method of trying on new
> ways of being. The characters I created were unfamiliar parts of
> myself.[5]

Here is a key to creative reclamation of parts of the psyche. The Tarot
objectifies what is already present but dormant. The spotlight of attention
and awareness serves to turn latency into potency. If you have already
employed the approaches suggested, you may use the same approach as a
spur for your own creativity. Enter the Tarot landscape of a chosen card
and just be open to the creative impulse. See, hear, touch, taste and smell
with your inner senses. Allow this experience to nourish your creative
spirit. Judith Bolinger expressed herself through poetry, you might do the
same.

The invitation to revision Tarot

> Tarot is now becoming a way of developing and increasing our
> access to intuition, honouring the intuitive reservoirs we all have
> within us, what native cultures call the four ways of seeing –
> vision, intuition, perception and insight.
>
> Angeles Arrien, *The Tarot Renaissance: Ancient
> Imagery for Contemporary Use*

Tarot presents us with archetypal hooks upon which we may hang
meaning. Our meaning need have no limit. Tarot can continue to serve us
in new and unexpected ways. We are only limited by the constraints of our
own imagination. The creative potential of Tarot has no limits. The
counselling and therapeutic value of Tarot's healing symbols is a new
avenue of development which is producing unexpected and interesting
interactions between client, Tarot and practitioner. Movement therapist
Susan K. Cole has correlated body movement posture with each of the
cards. As cards have been traditionally assigned planetary or elemental
correspondences so Susan Cole has assigned gestures, movements and
bodywork to each of the cards. For instance, in keeping with the airy
attribution given to the Lovers, the interaction here involves the breath
and learning how to give and receive support in reciprocal relationship.
The card of the Fool is associated with leaps and jumps. These

movements, of course, belong to the innocent and spontaneous play of childhood. But how often do adults jump for joy? Susan Cole uses a simple three-card reading which she calls 'The Flying Arrow' to represent a diagnostic picture of body, mind and spirit. She says:

> Tarot cards along with their symbolic interpretation are a means of identifying these obstacles and the level of awareness where they may exist.[6]

This of course is an innovative and creative extension of biodynamic bodywork and movement therapy.

Another innovative practitioner is Gail Fairfield who specialises in using the Tarot with people dealing with emotional pain in relationships. The Trumps become mirrors to the relationship. Accordingly the card of the Hanged Man asks partners to look at the situation in a new light. The Trump Temperance suggests a creative resolution. The Devil asks partners to own the shadow within. The Moon takes the relationship into inner needs. The Sun allows partners to comprehend these needs by the light of day. The Trump of the World shows the freedom and joy that comes from reaching self-integration. Additionally, Gail Fairfield uses Tarot with clients in recovery from addiction. The depth symbolism of the Tarot covers every human response and need.

In an altogether different field, management consultant Sharon Lerher uses Tarot in her work with companies. This is perhaps the most radical of the developments as Tarot has taken the leap from the humanities into the hard-headed world of commerce where decisions cost money. She uses a variety of spreads to gain insight into the dynamics of the company. She uses a circular spread with 14 segments to build a picture of the company. The headings are marketing, change, finances, balance, responsibility, relationships, management, leadership, environment, communication, risk taking, motivation, co-operation and innovation. There is, of course, nothing to prevent you from looking at your own workplace in exactly the same way. Lerher says:

> I have found the Tarot to be particularly effective for organisational application both because it provides access to a range of archetypal wisdom that is large and rich enough to reflect the complexity and uniqueness of organisational situations.[7]

Additionally she has modified the Celtic Cross spread to reflect the dynamics of a company. The spread is read in the following way:

Cards 1–6: the present state:

1 The heart of the organisation in the past.
2 The heart of the organisation in the present.
3 What the decision-makers are thinking about consciously.
4 The underlying issues of the organisation.
5 The organisation's creativity.
6 The organisation's ability to make decisions and set in motion its purposes, goals and actions.

Cards 7–10: the probable future:

7 Possibilities for innovation and creative breakthrough.
8 Staff relationships.
9 How the organisation handles the different polarities.
10 The business's natural expression.

This new departure can only be built on a company's willingness to incorporate intuitive information into the decision-making process and this is a bold step indeed. The fact that it has happened at all is something of a revolution. Perhaps the future will bring more bold steps.

We can only wonder where Tarot will go next. Wherever our vision will permit? These invitations are extended to you the reader and participant in this particular Tarot journey. You will have taken whatever you have needed. If you have interacted with the Tarot you will have begun to effect the process of your own awakening. Once begun this process never ceases. Like a butterfly emerging from the chrysalis of sleep, you too will emerge from yourself not once but endlessly. Tarot is a wise friend and gentle initiator. The Tarot teaches you to teach yourself. It is my hope that you have discovered this already and now know this to be true. Whatever you have begun here will be continued elsewhere for the Tarot journey is never complete after the first step has been taken.

NOTES

Chapter 1

1 Michael Dummett, *The Game of Tarot*, Duckworth, 1980, p. 172.
2 Stuart R. Kaplan, *The Encyclopaedia of Tarot*, Games Inc., 1978, p. 29.
3 Ibid., p. 69.
4 Ibid., p. 13.
5 Robert Wang, *An Introduction to the Golden Dawn Tarot*, Weiser, 1978, p. 13.
6 Unpublished lecture addressed to the Tomorrow Club in 1945 by Lady Harris, quoted in Robert Wang, *Qabalistic Tarot*, Weiser, 1983, p. 25.

Chapter 2

1 Robert Assagioli, *Psychosynthesis*, Turnstone Press, 1965, p. 217.
2 Ibid., p. 221.
3 Ibid., p. 218.
4 Ibid., p. 197.

Chapter 3

1 C.G. Jung, *Structure and Dynamics of the Psyche*, Routledge and Kegan Paul, 1960, p. 71.
2 David Whyte, *The Heart Aroused*, Doubleday, 1994, p. 235.
3 Assagioli, *Psychosynthesis*, p. 180.
4 Ibid., p. 177.
5 Ibid., p. 197.
6 Ibid., p. 204.

Chapter 5

1 A. Crowley, *The Book of Thoth*, Weiser, 1982, pp. 149–50.

Chapter 8

1 Jane English, 'A Scientist's Experience with Tarot', in James Wanless and Angeles Arrien (eds), *The Wheel of Tarot: A New Revolution*, Merrill-West, 1992, p. 16.
2 Ibid., p. 18.
3 Ibid., p. 22.
4 Wang, *Golden Dawn Tarot*, p. 104.

Chapter 9

1 Mary Greer and Rachel Pollack (eds), *New Thoughts on Tarot*, Newcastle Publishing Inc. Co., 1989, p. 5.
2 Assagioli, *Psychosynthesis*, p. 39.
3 Charloe Wittine, 'Tarot in the Therapeutic Process', in Wanless and Arrien (eds), *Wheel of Tarot*, p. 273.
4 Anne Stine, 'Archetypes, Tarot and Self Transformation', in Wanless and Arrien (eds), *Wheel of Tarot*, p. 167.
5 Judith Bolinger, 'From the Universe to the Empress', in Wanless and Arrien (eds), *Wheel of Tarot*, p. 217.
6 Susan K. Cole, 'Dance and Tarot', in Wanless and Arrien (eds), *Wheel of Tarot*, p. 205.
7 Sharon Lerher, 'Organizational Management through Tarot Symbolism', in Wanless and Arrien (eds), *Wheel of Tarot*, p. 250.

FURTHER READING

Practical

Fenton, Sasha, *Tarot in Action*, Aquarian Press, 1987.
Fenton, Sasha, *Super Tarot*, Aquarian Press, 1991.

General

Almond, Jocelyn and Keith Seddon, *Tarot for Relationships*, Aquarian
  Press, 1990.
Connolly, Eileen, *Tarot: A New Handbook for the Apprentice*, Aquarian
  Press, 1986.
Connolly, Eileen, *Tarot: The Handbook for the Journeyman*, Aquarian
  Press, 1990.
Kaplan, Stuart R., *The Encyclopaedia of Tarot*, Games Inc., 1978.
Dummett, Michael, *The Game of Tarot*, Duckworth, 1980.
Pollack, Rachel, *Seventy Eight Degrees of Wisdom*, Vols 1 and 2,
  Aquarian Press, 1983.
Pollack, Rachel, *Tarot Readings and Meditations*, Aquarian Press, 1990.

Western Mystery perspective

Hoeller, Stephan A., *The Royal Road: A Manual of Kabbalistic Meditation
  on the Tarot*, Quest Books, 1975.
Knight, Gareth, *The Treasure House of Images*, Aquarian Press, 1986.
Ozaniec, Naomi, *The Element Tarot Handbook: Initiation into the Key
  Elements of Tarot*, Element Books, 1994.
Wang, Robert, *An Introduction to the Golden Dawn Tarot*, Weiser, 1978.
Wang, Robert, *Qabalistic Tarot*, Weiser, 1983.
Willis, Tony, *The Magick and the Tarot*, Aquarian Press, 1988.

Jungian perspective

Hamaker-Zondag, Karen, *Tarot as a Way of Life: A Jungian Approach to Tarot*, Weiser, 1977.

Anthologies

Greer, Mary and Rachel Pollack (eds), *New Thoughts on Tarot*, Newcastle Publishing Co. Inc., 1989.

Wanless, James and Angeles Arrien (eds), *Wheel of Tarot: A New Revolution*, Merrill-West, 1992.

INDEX

Other related titles

TEACH YOURSELF

MEDITATION

Naomi Ozaniec

Meditation is a traditional discipline which has been practised through the ages, and has long been recognised for its spiritual and restorative powers.

Teach Yourself Meditation introduces the theory and practice of meditation in a direct and simple manner. The book includes a variety of approaches, and compares the methods and goals of both Eastern and Western systems. With its holistic view of life, meditation can help you to gain a new perspective for the future.

Naomi Ozaniec has studied meditation for over ten years and has written several books on the subject.

TEACH YOURSELF

VISUALIZATION

Pauline Wills

Visualization, the carrying of a clear visual image in the mind, has long been accepted in the East as playing an important role in balancing and maintaining the mind-body-spirit relationship.

This book will show you how to practise the techniques, using simple, clearly illustrated exercises, to relieve stress, alleviate specific health problems and increase your sense of well-being – in your personal relationships, at work, and in all aspects of your everyday life. The book includes a selection of mandalas which you can use in your quest for personal growth.

Pauline Wills first trained as a nurse. She subsequently developed an interest in complementary therapies, and now uses visualization alongside a wide range of other treatments. She has written extensively on reflexology and colour therapy.

TEACH YOURSELF

ASTROLOGY
Third Edition

Jeff Mayo

A revised and updated edition of a classic textbook, *Teach Yourself Astrology* tells you all you need to know about this fascinating subject.

Jeff Mayo draws on his vast experience as an internationally successful teacher and consultant in astrology. He provides not only a vivid introduction for the reader who wants to learn the basics of the art, but also presents the practicing astrologer with a fresh insight into a birth-chart through a new and unique system of personality interpretation.

Jeff has been assisted in the revision of this exciting new volume by Christine Ramsdale who has extensive teaching and consultative experience in the field of astrology.

CHINESE ASTROLOGY

Richard Craze
with Billy Lee

Teach Yourself Chinese Astrology is a clear and practical guide which explains how this ancient and well-tested system of astrology works. The basic idea is that people are classified according to certain fundamental types, which are described by twelve animals and relate to the year of birth. This book will show you how to construct and interpret your own personal and unique Chinese astrological charts, as well as the charts of your friends and family.

Not only can you find out what animal you are and what it means in Chinese astrology, but you can also discover your secret animal and how it can help you improve your career, relationships, health and luck. Whether you are a dragon, a monkey or snake by birth year, it is certain that you are never just one animal, but a combination of several – the fascinating part is finding out which ones!

Richard Craze is a freelance writer, specializing in books on Chinese culture, the New Age and religion. Billy Lee is a Chinese astrologer and Tai Ch'i teacher.

Other related titles

TEACH YOURSELF

EASTERN PHILOSOPHY

Mel Thompson

This book examines the key ideas that developed within the ancient civilisations of India and China. It presents a range of philosophies that both inform discussion of personal, moral and social issues, and also address the fundamental questions about the nature of reality and the place and purpose of human life within it.

From the exotic images of sexual Tantra to the simple precision of Zen, or from the social order in traditional Confucian teaching to the rich variety of Hindu ideas and lifestyles, Eastern Philosophy provides a feast of ideas of universal relevance.

- looks at the ethical and social implications of Eastern Philosophy
- all key terms are given in their original language and are fully explained
- points to parallels with Western thought, where appropriate
- provides essential background information for appreciating the religions of India and the Far East

Dr Mel Thompson is a freelance writer and editor, specialising in philosophy, religion and ethics.

TEACH YOURSELF

FENG SHUI

Richard Craze & Roni Jay

Feng Shui is the ancient Chinese art of arranging your surroundings to receive maximum benefit from good 'ch'i' – universal energy. In *Teach Yourself Feng Shui* the authors explain in a clear and practical way how this popular subject can be learnt and utilised at home, at work and in the garden.

The book covers:

- ■ the history and principles of Feng Shui
- ■ the practical application of Feng Shui
- ■ how to use Feng Shui to influence your relationships, money, health and children.

Richard Craze and Roni Jay are both professional writers for various subjects including New Age and Alternative Health and they have written extensively on Feng Shui.